TURBO

TURBO

AN A-Z OF TURBOCHARGED CARS

NEW BURLINGTON BOOKS

GRAHAM ROBSON

A QUINTET BOOK

Published by New Burlington Books
6 Blundell Street
London N7 9BH

ISBN 1-85348-043-6

This book was designed and produced by
Quintet Publishing Limited
6 Blundell Street
London N7 9BH

Art Director: Peter Bridgewater
Designer: Stuart Walden
Editor: Shaun Barrington

Typeset in Great Britain by
Central Southern Typesetters, Eastbourne
Manufactured in Hong Kong by
Regent Publishing Services Limited
Printed in Hong Kong by
Leefung-Asco Printers Limited

CONTENTS

Introduction	6
Supercharging before Turbocharging	10
Alpine Renault GTA	14
Audi Quattro Coupe	16
Bentley Mulsanne	20
BMW 2002	22
BMW 745i	26
Chevrolet Corvair Monza Spyder	30
Chrysler Maserati	32
Citroen CX25 GTI	34
Dodge Daytona	36
Ferrari F1	38
Ferrari GTO	40
Fiat 124 Spider	42
Ford Escort RS	44
Ford Capri 2.8	46
Ford Sierra RS Cosworth	48
Ford RS200	52
Ford Mustang	56
Ford Thunderbird Coupe	58
Indy racing car (DFX engine)	60
Lancia Delta S4	62
Lancia Delta HF 4WD	64
Lotus Esprit	68
Maserati BiTurbo	72
Mazda 323 4WD	74
Mazda RX-7 2.6	76
Mercedes-Benz 300TD	78
Merkur XR4Ti	80
MG Metro	82
Mitsubishi Colt Starion	86
Nissan Fairlady Z/300ZX	88
Oldsmobile F85 Jetfire	90
Peugeot 205 Turbo 16	92
Porsche 911	96
Porsche 924	98
Porsche 944	100
Porsche 956 Group C Sports Car	102
Porsche 959	104
Range Rover TD	106
Renault 5 Turbo	110
Renault 5 GT Turbo	112
Saab 99/900	114
Saab 9000	116
Toyota Celica Twin-Cam	118
TVR	120
Volvo 760	122
Index	126

INTRODUCTION

The turbocharged car, and the high-performance image which goes with it, is a phenomenon of the 1970s and 1980s. Harnessing in the energy of the exhaust gases of a car engine, which would otherwise go to waste, has allowed designers to make small cars go faster and to turn sports cars into Supercars.

There are pundits who insist that turbocharging is a passing fashion and that normally-aspirated multi-valve engines will take over instead. Such views fly in the face of the facts – for nothing beats turbocharging as a way of boosting the power of an ordinary engine by such an enormous amount. With a turbo, the power of a road-car engine can often be increased by 50 or even 100 per cent, but multi-valve engines are scratching to add any more than 25 per cent. In competition cars the

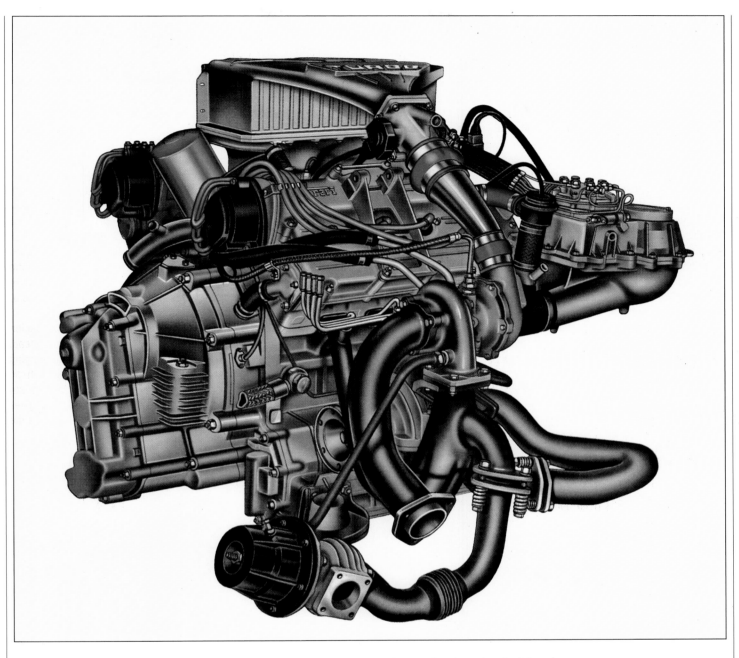

LEFT In the 1950s and 1960s, cars with 'blown' engines had superchargers, and were extrovert machinery. This was a specially modified Chevrolet Corvette.

INSET, LEFT On this Corvette V8 engine, the supercharger sat between the cylinder banks, with carburettors on top of it: *not* a compact, nor neat, installation!

ABOVE Turbocharging, 1980s style, by Ferrari. This GTO-type V8 engine has the turbocharger mounted neatly to one side of the engine, with fuel injection, and is a little more bulky than the normally-aspirated unit. Power for free? Almost . . .

'unfair advantage' is so enormous that the sport's rulers often legislate them out of existence!

Not only that, but most turbocharged cars seem to have truly exuberant characters. A normally-aspirated car can be very fast and one with a multi-valve engine can be even faster and can make all the right noises – but there is nothing to beat the exhilarating surge of power which follows the cutting-in of power in a turbocharged car.

Admittedly, earlier cars did not respond as instantly as they should have done, but there was even something wickedly spine-tingling about the way one floored the throttle, waited a second or so for the 'turbo lag' to disappear as the whistle of the turbocharger built up, and went on to harness the extra thrust which then appeared. In the same way it is stimulating to drive quickly along a winding road in a turbo car, shifting up and down through the gears, going on and coming off the throttle, and hearing the flutter of the wastegate control every time it operates.

No wonder the 'go faster' accessory shops now sell 'Turbo' badges in large numbers – but not turbocharger kits – sometimes for cars whose engines are so old, or so badly designed, that they would surely split asunder if boosted!

Turbocharged engines have now been fitted to so many of the world's cars that it would be impossible to describe every one. All that can be done, in this book, is to give the reader a flavour of the market place and to pick out the most significant models.

The between-Wars vogue in supercharged cars was over by the end of the 1930s, and it was some time before turbocharged automotive engines were first developed (during the 1950s), with the world's largest car-maker, General Motors, in the lead. Early in 1962 that corporation launched the world's original turbocharged cars – the rear-engined Chevrolet Corvair Monza Spider, and the V8 front-engined Oldsmobile Jetfire.

At the time, there was no rush to join, or beat 'The General', so it was not until 1969 that BMW began to race a turbocharged version of its 2002 saloon. Early in the 1970s Porsche also began to apply turbocharging to some of its racing cars (notably to the fabulously fast and successful flat 12 engine of the 917) and several specialist companies, notably Broadspeed in the UK, began to develop turbocharging conversion kits for mundane family cars.

The European breakthrough came from BMW in 1973 – ironically enough it was *exactly* at the time that the Yom Kippur War and the first energy crisis saw oil prices go through the roof! BMW's 2002 Turbo was only on sale for a year but it was speedily followed by Porsche's fabulous 911 Turbo.

Sales of Porsche Turbos began in 1975, this certainly being a major influence on the rest of the world's motor industry. If the world's most meticulous developer of cars thought that turbochargers were ripe for use, other manufacturers were ready to follow. Saab was the first to put a series-production turbo saloon on sale. The fact that Cosworth's turbocharged DFX engine started to dominate North American motor racing from 1976, and that Renault built the world's first turbocharged Formula One car a year later, must both have helped.

General Motors went down the turbocharging trail in a big way for its 1978 models, with turbocharged V6 units, while Ford-USA followed them a year later with its turbocharged four-cylinder 'Lima' designs. The final seal of approval for turbocharging came in 1982, when Britain's most conservative concern, Rolls-Royce, announced the Bentley Mulsanne Turbo.

By that time turbo-engines were listed by Audi, Bentley, BMW, Buick, Fiat, Ford-USA, Ford-Europe, Lotus, Maserati, Mercedes-Benz, Mitsubishi, Nissan, Peugeot, Porsche, Renault, Saab, Toyota and Volvo, and many more followed in the next few years.

Perhaps the boom in turbocharged cars is already at its height. What advances may be made in the 1990s?

BELOW The first modern turbocharged F1 car was produced in the late 1970s by Renault. The engine was a V6 unit, and the turbocharger can be seen mounted low down, and to the right. In 1977 the peak output of 1½-litre F1 engines was about 550 bhp; by the mid-1980s peak ratings had increased to no less than 1,200 bhp in 'qualifying' form, and more than 900 bhp for the races themselves.

OPPOSITE In 1931, Vittorio Jano's masterpiece, the eight-cylinder Alfa Romeo 8C2300 was produced. This had a supercharged unit like all the great competition cars (sports or Grand Prix machines) of the day. Turbocharging did not take over until the 1970s.

SUPERCHARGING BEFORE TURBOCHARGING

There are two types of motor car engine – atmospheric or 'blown'. Atmospheric engines get no help with pulling fuel/air mixture into their cylinders, whereas 'blown' engines have it forced in at high pressure. Because of this, a 'blown' engine gets more than its fair share of air and can produce a lot more power.

The principle of the internal combustion engine is well known. Air is propelled into the cylinders from the outside, mixed with fuel, compressed, exploded, then pushed out through the exhaust system. The explosion creates energy, which is used to turn a crankshaft and produce power to drive the vehicle.

For many years after motor cars were invented all used what we now call 'normally aspirated' or 'atmospheric' engines, where the fuel-air mixture is drawn in to the cylinders by the suction of descending pistons. Some engines were more efficient than others, because the shaping of

inlet and exhaust manifolds, along with the detailing of gas passages inside the cylinder heads, was an art (rather than a science) not correctly practised by everyone. If the air supply is restricted or is of reduced density (as at high altitude), the engine power falls away.

Racing car designers soon realised that there was one easy way to produce more power, that being to burn more oxygen. This could either be done by giving the engine bigger lungs (by increasing its capacity), or by getting more air into the same engine.

Bigger engines were usually heavier engines, which was undesirable. Logic then suggested that more air could only be forced into the engine by using a pump of some sort or another.

The first type of 'pump' to be used in piston engines – for cars and more especially for aircraft – was the supercharger, the name being self-explanatory. There were many types but all were mechanically driven

from the engine's crankshaft, by a belt, chain, or even by gearing. Extra power was developed, even from low engine speeds, but a considerable amount of that power was needed to drive the pump. The result was that supercharged engines tended to be *less* powerful than 'atmospheric' engines at low speeds, but much more powerful at the 'top end'.

The first superchargers were used in aircraft during the First World War, and it was Mercedes who announced the first supercharged road cars in 1921. The first 'blown' Grand Prix car win came in 1923 and until 1951 this type of engine reigned supreme.

A *turbocharger* is not mechanically connected to the engine but is driven by it. It has a small centrifugal compressor and a radial-flow turbine, which are mounted on a common axial shaft. The turbocharger is fitted on the engine's exhaust manifold, the turbine is propelled by the exhaust gases and the compressor pushes boosted air into the engine. In this way a turbocharger uses the otherwise wasted energy of the exhaust gases, and there is a greatly increased flow of air into the engine in almost every way then, this is 'power for free'.

Usually a turbocharger can produce much more high-pressure air than the engine can use, so all manner of sophisticated 'add-on' controls are used to keep the pressure, and supply, within the limits that the engine can take.

Usually the amount of air which can be passed is limited by the size of the inlet trunking, and by the turbocharger itself. A classic case is the British Ford Sierra RS Cosworth, its 122 CID/2.0 litre engine is rated at 204 bhp for road use, that can be tuned to about 340 bhp for flat-out racing applications. The same engine, when fitted with a larger turbocharger and air passages, and modified fuel injection systems, can be boosted to around 450 bhp.

high a pressure. All modern systems therefore tend to have what is known as a 'wastegate' control, literally a safety valve set to 'blow off' when the pressure exceeds a certain level. Sophisticated engine control systems sometimes 'tune' the wastegate to operate at different pressures for different engine speeds, and to cut down on the available boost as engine speeds rise towards the mechanical limits.

Air which has been compressed rapidly, as in a turbocharger, tends to be hot. Many cars now have their boosted air fed through charge intercoolers on its way to the engine. Such coolers, almost invariably radiators mounted in an air-stream, cool the air to make it more dense than before, and give the engine a chance to develop even more power than it might have done.

Turbochargers were invented, in principle, by a Swiss engineer, Dr Alfred Buchi, who patented an exhaust-driven piston-type supercharger for diesel engines in 1905. The piston type was soon superseded by exhaust driven fans and thus the modern turbocharger was born.

The earliest successful turbocharged petrol engines were aircraft types produced during the Second World War by the American Alison, and Pratt & Whitney concerns. It was the suppliers for those companies, notably Garrett AiResearch, who developed smaller units and applied them successfully to stationary and commercial vehicle diesel power units.

It is important to remember that although turbochargers effectively give a car designer 'free power', they are also demanding units which give themselves, and their surroundings, a very hard time. Because they are small, with very low inertia, and have to deal with large volumes of gases, they have to resolve very quickly indeed. At full blast a small auto-type turbocharger might be spinning at more than 100,000 or even 150,000 rpm – and it must be capable of reaching these speeds very rapidly indeed after the car's throttle pedal has suddenly been floored.

The main problems with turbochargers centre on lubrication, cooling, and balancing, but extended experience in use (sometimes at extremely high specific outputs as in Formula One racing cars) has made the modern generation of turbos very reliable indeed. Although superchargers have not completely died out, there is no question that the turbocharger has completely won the battle. No other cost-effective solution to pressure charging is yet in sight.

OPPOSITE Somehow you expected a magnificently styled 1930s Bugatti like this to have an ultra-powerful supercharged engine. The engine bay was full of carefully-finished eight cylinder engine, with the mechanically driven supercharger fixed to the right side.

BELOW Italian F1 GP, 1933, with Fagioli's Tipo B (also known as P3) Alfa Romeo single seater in the pits for refuelling. Power was by courtesy of a 2.6-litre supercharged eight-cylinder twin-cam engine. Peak power was about 215 bhp.

ALPINE RENAULT
GTA V6 TURBO

PRODUCTION SPAN
Introduced 1985
-
ENGINE
V6 cyl, ohc
-
CAPACITY
150 CID/2,458cc
-
MAXIMUM POWER
200 bhp
-
CHASSIS/SUSPENSION
Steel backbone chassis
frame, coil spring/
wishbone ifs, coil spring/
wishbone irs
-
BODY STYLE
2 door 2+2 seater coupé
-
TOP SPEED
149mph/238kph
-
0-60MPH
6.3 seconds
-

Way back in the 1950s, Alpines were simple rear-engined sports cars built by a Renault dealer in Dieppe. In the 1960s and 1970s the Alpine-Renault business grew considerably, and by the 1980s it had been bought up by the Renault concern. The GTA was the first new model produced under Renault ownership and was considerably more 'up-market' than any previous Alpine-Renault.

The GTA was really an up-date of the long established Type 310 model. Like the A310 it used a steel backbone chassis with the engine in the extreme tail, it had a body shell moulded from glass-fibre and it used a developed version of the same PRV V6 engine. The novelty of this particular Alpine-Renault, apart from its new style, was that there were alternative engine sizes and tunes, one of them being normally aspirated the other being a turbocharged unit.

Compared with the old A310, for which the GTA was a direct replacement, the new car was larger and roomier in all respects – it had a three inch longer wheelbase, was four inches wider and two inches higher, all of which helped to make the cabin more spacious. Not only that, the new car was beautiful and was aerodynamically very efficient, with a claimed coefficient of drag (Cd) of only 0.28.

The structure of the GTA was more integrated than before, for although the steel backbone frame used thinner-section metal than before, the body shell was moulded rather than bolted to that frame. In effect this made the GTA a steel glass reinforced plastic (GRP) monocoque, and a sturdy one at that for it weighed in at about 2,618lb/1,187kg.

The V6 engines used in the GTA were the latest derivatives of the design jointly developed by Peugeot, Renault and Volvo in the 1970s, and used in cars as diverse as the Volvo 760 and the DeLorean DMC12. By the early 1980s turbocharged versions had been put on sale in the Renault 25 executive model, and it was a further modified version which was one of those offered for the GTA.

The normally-aspirated engine used in the GTA was a 160bhp 174 CID/2,849cc unit, but the turbocharged engine developed 200bhp from only 150 CID/2,458cc – it was in other words, smaller but more efficient; the Renault 25 Turbo engine developed 182bhp. Not only was a Garrett AiResearch T3 turbocharger fitted, but there was an air-to-air intercooler, fuel injection, all integrated by a fully-mapped Renix engine management system.

It was an impressive and extremely reliable power unit which, matched to an all-direct five-speed transmission, allowed the GTA Turbo to reach nearly 150mph/240kph, and still record over 20 (Imperial) mpg.

All in all the GTA was a very impressive package, with four-wheel disc brakes, power-assisted rack and pinion steering, and a very well equipped interior. Like Porsche's 911 however there was no disguising the fact that it had a heavy engine in the extreme tail, and even the use of much wider-section rear tyres than those used at the front could not 'kill' the oversteering tendencies.

On the open road however, the GTA was a smart, very fast, and well packaged machine, one with which Renault hoped to penetrate the North American market.

RIGHT Compared with its predecessor, the Alpine-Renault GTA was in a much smoother and more integrated style. From this view it is difficult to realize that the engine is in the extreme tail. GTAs had flashing performance, and – in spite of a rearward weight-bias – very predictable roadholding. The body shell was in glass fibre, which hid a steel backbone chassis frame.

BELOW RIGHT From this angle there is no mistaking the engine fitted to the GTA – a turbocharged V6. This was a developed version of the PRV design first used in Volvos and Renaults of the mid-1970s, which had a 90-degree vee angle, and single overhead valve gear. The style, and the cooling arrangements, were so thoughtfully completed that there is no clue to the rear mounting of this engine.

AUDI QUATTRO COUPE

PRODUCTION SPAN
Introduced 1980
-
ENGINE
5 cyl, ohc
-
CAPACITY
131 CID/2,144cc
-
MAXIMUM POWER
200 bhp
-
CHASSIS/SUSPENSION
Unit-construction steel
body/chassis structure,
coil spring/MacPherson
strut ifs, coil spring/
MacPherson strut irs
-
BODY STYLE
2 door 4 seater coupé
-
TOP SPEED
132mph/211kph
-
0-60MPH
7.8 seconds
-

The original Audi Quattro of 1980 will go down in motoring history as the car which sparked off the fashion for four-wheel-drive – both in the showrooms and in World Championship rallying. By any standards the Quattro, and its descendants, were extremely successful as road cars and as rally cars.

In fact this was one of those rare modern cars which was the brain-wave of an individual engineer before it was formally adopted by the factory planners. Walter Treser of Audi originally mated the four-wheel-drive transmission of the Audi-VW Iltis off-road, soft-skin military vehicle to the normally front-drive Audi 80 saloon, demonstrated its agility to his superiors, and saw it adopted as an official project. The result was not only the birth of the 200bhp Quattro Coupé, but of a whole interrelated range of four-wheel-drive Audi passenger cars.

Like many other cars covered in this book, the turbocharged engine used in the Quattro turned a good car into an outstanding machine. Until that point the fastest Audis of the 1970s had used front-wheel-drive layouts with 131 CID/2.2 litre five-cylinder engines, the most powerful of which produced about 136 bhp. These had very simple cylinder head designs, with inlet and exhaust ports on the same side of the head. Such engines were planned for use in a new generation of cars, which included a smart coupé.

Almost from the start it seems Audi decided to produce its four-wheel-drive Quattro (the name of course is Italian for four) with an extremely powerful engine, and to use it in rallies, in which four-wheel-drive cars were finally made eligible. With the aid of fuel injection and a KKK turbocharger the refined five-cylinder engine was turned into a very broad-shouldered super-sports unit, and the standard road car was given 200bhp, and a top speed of around 135mph/216kph.

In the Quattro the engine was mounted well forward, ahead of the line of the front-wheels, with the cylinder block leaning over towards the right side of the engine bay, and with the water-cooling radiator mounted on the left side of the bay. The turbocharger was under the exhaust manifold on the right side with an air-to-air intercooler ahead of it, immediately behind the front grille.

Compared with the front-drive Coupé, the styling of the turbocharged car was modified so that flared wheel arches covered wide-rim wheels, while the four-wheel-drive installation meant that a new type of independent rear suspension also had to be fitted. In spite of its nose-heavy weight distribution and a degree of engine turbo lag, the Quattro was an impressive road car which Audi began to make at the rate of 10 cars a day.

From 1981 the Quattro was an overwhelmingly successful rally car, first with a 300bhp, and later with a 330bhp power unit. A 200-off short-wheelbase Quattro Sport was also built in 1984–85, in which a special twin-cam 4 valves/cylinder version of the engine was fitted. In road car form these had 306bhp, but in white hot rally car guise up to 450bhp was available!

The Quattro's technicalities made a fascinating study for motoring enthusiasts. Not only was it a four-wheel-drive car, but there was a turbocharged *five*-cylinder engine way ahead of the line of the front wheels. The Quattro, therefore, was the first of the 1980s generation of four-wheel-drive supercars. Its styling was fresh in 1980, and still unmistakable seven or eight years later.

ABOVE In Audi language, Quattro means four-wheel-drive, but the flared wheel arches and wide-rimmed alloy wheels mean that this is the 132mph turbocharged model.

RIGHT The Quattro's styling was by an Englishman, Martin Smith, the basic body structure being shared with that of the non-turbocharged two- and four-wheel- drive coupes. The engine sat ahead of the front wheels, and there was compact four- seater accommodation.

LEFT Even though it could exceed 130mph, the Quattro was a full four-seater coupe.

TOP Audi's famous four-ring badge stems from its membership of the four-marque Auto-Union family – Auto, DKW, Horch and Wanderer – a merger set up in Germany in the 1930s.

ABOVE Later model Quattros were given electronic instrument displays. The rev-counter is saying nothing at this stage, but the 200bhp turbocharged engine can be urged to 6,000rpm and beyond.

BELOW This was the complex engine bay revealed to the Quattro owner when he opened the bonnet. The five-cylinder engine was tilted to the right side of the engine bay, and the turbocharger was hidden under the manifolding.

BENTLEY
MULSANNE
TURBO R

PRODUCTION SPAN
Introduced 1986
—
ENGINE
V8 cyl, ohv
—
CAPACITY
412 CID/6,750cc
—
MAXIMUM POWER
330 bhp (estimated –
see text)
—
CHASSIS/SUSPENSION
Unit-construction steel
body/chassis structure,
coil spring/wishbone
arm ifs, coil spring/semi-
trailing arm irs, with
self-levelling
—
BODY STYLE
4 door 5 seater saloon
—
TOP SPEED
143mph/229kph
—
0-60MPH
7.0 seconds
—

It is ironic that the arrival of a turbocharged Rolls-Royce (badged as a Bentley in fact) seemed to give respectability to the entire turbo-charging cult. Although it had been years since Rolls-Royce really *had* built the 'Best Car in the World', the company was still respected for the calibre of its very careful development programmes. Even though it arrived years later than many other turbocharged models, the fact that Rolls-Royce had spent nearly a decade 'getting it right' somehow re-assured everyone.

The new car was badged as a Bentley Mulsanne Turbo when launched in 1982, and was upgraded to 'Turbo R' in 1986 with a power boost, fuel injection and much more sporty roadholding. The original Mulsanne was 'a massive and extremely expensive saloon car, which had been launched in 1980, and was itself a completely restyled version of the Bentley T-Series/Rolls-Royce Silver Shadow model which had been on the market since 1965.

Rolls-Royce like to get things absolutely right before launching a new car (at least this is the image the company likes to maintain) and hangs on to existing machinery for a long time. In 1965 the Silver Shadow/T-Series was the first ever car from Crewe to have a monocoque structure, all-independent suspension and disc brakes; its V8 engine had been put on sale in a previous model in 1959.

A turbocharged car (which was badged as a 'Bentley' because this was the more overtly sporting of the two marques) was inspired by chief executive David Plastow in the early 1970s, and at first was really no more than a 'conversion' of the existing saloon. It was not until a new management generation set out to rejuvenate Bentley's image that the suspension was completely reworked to give a firmer ride and more responsive steering. The 1986 model, therefore, was 'Turbo R', with the 'R' denoting 'Roadholding'. Cynics suggested that the car simply had not had any roadholding before this . . .

Because the Bentley's engine was a large 412 CID/6,750cc unit, when the turbocharged version was produced a large turbo was needed to do a proper job. In this case a TO4 Garrett AiResearch unit was chosen, mounted to the right, and ahead of, the engine. There was, and still is, no intercooler.

From 1982 to 1986 the boosted air was fed to a four-barrel Solex carburettor sitting atop the engine, but for 1987 (and with increased power and better exhaust emission control in mind) a Bosch KE fuel-injection system was fitted instead. Although Rolls-Royce/Bentley have never revealed engine power outputs in the UK, modern West German legislation obliged them to relent in the 1980s. The original carburettor/turbo produced 298bhp (DIN), whereas the fuel-injected/turbo produced 328bhp, neither being outstanding, but both were blessed with copious torque at very low revs.

Although the Turbo R had supercar-like performance, it was nevertheless a superbly equipped and finished saloon car, so expensive as to be affordable by only a few hundred customers a year. Because automatic transmission was standard and the sound insulation was carefully arranged it was often easy to ignore the presence of a turbo completely.

TOP RIGHT When Rolls-Royce put the Bentley Mulsanne Turbo on sale in 1982, it was the finest accolade that turbocharging could gain. There are discreet 'Turbo' badges to give the game away – the only other sign being the impressive way the car performed. This was a 1985 model, from which the Turbo R developed a year later.

BELOW The Turbo R kept the same restrained body style as other cars in the Rolls-Royce Silver Spirit/Bentley Mulsanne family. This was the Turbo R, as revealed in 1986; like other turbocharged Bentleys it had a painted, rather than polished stainless steel, radiator shell. The Turbo's top speed was well over 140mph.

BMW 2002 TURBO

PRODUCTION SPAN
1973 and 1974

ENGINE
4 cyl, ohc

CAPACITY
121 CID/1,990cc

MAXIMUM POWER
170 bhp

CHASSIS/SUSPENSION
Unit-construction body/
chassis structure, coil
spring/MacPherson strut
ifs, coil spring/semi-
trailing arm irs

BODY STYLE
2 door 4 seater saloon

TOP SPEED
130mph/208kph

0-60MPH
7.3 seconds

Until the late 1960s BMW had absolutely no experience of turbo-charged engines. In the 1930s and 1940s the company had built a series of successful supercharged aero-engines, but this was no longer relevant a full design generation later.

In the 1950s and early 1960s BMW struggled to stay in business, but the tide turned in 1962. In that year the first of a new generation of middle-size, middle-class cars, the four-cylinder engined 1500, went on sale. It was immediately popular and put the Bavarian company back on the path to greatness. The secret of this car's success was an advanced, and rugged, four-cylinder engine with overhead camshaft valve gear.

Four years later a slightly smaller saloon, the 1600–2, was launched, also using the same engine. In the next few years this design developed into a complete range – 1600TI, 1802, 2002, 2002 ti, 2000 tii, and finally the 2002 Turbo. Unfortunately the turbocharged derivative appeared at exactly the wrong time – in 1973, when the Yom Kippur war and the subsequent Energy Crisis upset the world of performance car motoring – and it was on sale for only a year.

The 2002 turbo's engine was a 122 CID/2 litre version of the famous four-cylinder unit which had been revealed in 1961. In the 1960s BMW proved its worth by super-tuning it for use in sports racing and single-seater racing cars. In the 1970s it was also treated to a new 16 valve cylinder head, and became a race-winning unit at Formula 2 level. Later on, turbocharged versions of this engine were fitted to Brabham Formula 1 cars.

The original turbocharged engine was designed as a racing unit, first campaigned in 2002 saloons in 1969, and was good enough to win its capacity class in that year's European Touring Car Championship. It was the first turbocharged engine ever to start a European motor race. Its refinement for production car use took another three years.

In comparison with later turbo packages this early-1970s BMW engine was inflexible and rather peaky. The KKK turbo was mounted low down on the right side of the engine, under the exhaust manifold, and fed the inlet manifold through a long pipe routed up and over the top of the cam cover; there was no intercooler. At low rpm there was no perceptible turbo effect, and testers found that the real power appeared with a rush at about 4,000 rpm; maximum boost was 8 psi/0.55 Bar.

There had been no problem in producing 170bhp, for the 1969-model race cars had developed well over 200bhp, and the sensational mid-engined BMW Turbo show car of 1972 was rated at 200bhp. The problems at that time were in taming the engine – particularly in terms of turbo lag – and generally making this an easier car to drive.

To match the much increased power of the engine (170bhp instead of the normally-aspirated 2002 tii's 130bhp) the chassis was given venti-lated front disc brakes, lowered and firmed-up suspension, with 5.5in wheel rims and 185/70VR 13in tyres. Flared wheel arches, a boot lid spoiler and a deep under-bumper spoiler were all added to the shell to improve the aerodynamics.

When it was launched the car also carried '2002 turbo' script in mirror-image writing on the spoiler, but this was thought to be aggres-sive and was soon deleted following heavy criticism from the German motoring press.

This pioneering BMW – Europe's very first turbocharged production car – was only in production for ten months. Only 1,672 such cars were built, and BMW limped out of this market sector for some years.

RIGHT In 1973, BMW's 2002 Turbo was the first turbocharged saloon car to go on sale in Europe, but it was launched as the energy crisis struck the motor industry. The first turbocharged BMWs had raced successfully in 1969. This limited-production model not only had a 170bhp engine, but all-independent suspension and ventilated front-wheel disc brakes.

BELOW RIGHT Early BMW 2002 Turbos had the word 'turbo' in reversed script on the steep front spoiler, but later models like this restored example were a little more discreet. Considering the car's 130mph top speed, there seemed to be a distinct lack of headlamp power for night-time motoring!

ABOVE When BMW produced the turbocharged version of the 2002, it also attended to the chassis and the aerodynamics. The wheel arch extensions were to cover widened wheels, and there was a boot lid spoiler to aid high-speed stability.

RIGHT The 2002's turbocharger was hidden away on the right (far) side of the engine bay, pressurized air being fed to the shapely inlet manifolds across the front of the engine.

ABOVE LEFT The all-important turbocharger boost gauge was in an auxiliary panel in the centre of the facia. Except for its padded steering wheel, the turbo's driving layout was much like that of less powerful 1602/2002 family models.

ABOVE One of the most famous, and quite unmistakable, badges in the world of motoring is always linked to BMW's kidney-style grille motif. So it was on the 2002 Turbo.

LEFT Cast alloy wheels, fat tyres, and wheel arch extensions hint at the purpose of the car – the 'turbo' decal on the nearby panel confirms it.

BMW 745i

PRODUCTION SPAN
1980 to 1986

ENGINE
6 cyl, ohc

CAPACITY
196 CID/3,210cc

MAXIMUM POWER
252bhp

CHASSIS/SUSPENSION
Unit-construction body/
chassis structure, coil
spring/MacPherson strut
ifs, coil spring/semi-
trailing arm irs

BODY STYLE
4 door 5 seater saloon

TOP SPEED
137mph/219kph

0-60MPH
7.3 seconds

After BMW dropped the 2002 Turbo at the end of 1974, the company said it had no intention of building another turbocharged road car, though development for motorsport purposes would continue. Its mid-engined M1 coupé had a normally-aspirated six-cylinder unit with four valves per cylinder, as did other projected 'M' derivatives.

Then, at the end of the 1970s, BMW needed a 'flagship' derivative of the bulky new 7-Series models, and the turbo option was re-examined. The result was that a gloriously fast and well equipped executive saloon, the 745i, was launched in 1980 and was built in limited numbers for the next six years. Because of the layout of components in the engine bay the 745i was never built with right-hand steering.

Just to confuse the issue BMW (South Africa) also sold a 745i model, but this had the M1's normally aspirated 286bhp engine!

After BMW's technical and financial rebirth in the 1960s its first six-cylinder engined saloon was the 2800 model of 1968, and this was replaced by the much improved 7-Series range of 1977. At first these cars had 171, 183 and 201 CID (2.8, 3.0 and 3.3 litres) but later 195 and 214 CID (3.2 and 3.5 litre) engines were also developed. It was on the basis of the rationalised 195 CID/3.2 litre 'six' that a turbocharged car, the 745i, was developed.

BMW's usual model-naming policy – such as 732i – denoted a 7-Series car with a particular engine size and with fuel injection. The turbo-car's title of 745i however made no sense by this standard – BMW's excuse was that to turbocharge the 195 CID/3.2 litre unit made it the equivalent of a 275 CID/4.5 litre engine instead, and hence the '745i' badge!

The big six-cylinder engine was a direct development of the overhead-cam four which had been used in the 2002 Turbo and was a smooth and extremely reliable seven-main-bearing unit. As with the 2002 Turbo therefore the 745i's engine was essentially a 'conversion'.

In the years which separated the 2002 Turbo from the 745i, turbo technology (and in particular the matching of turbocharger behaviour to the engine) had advanced considerably. The turbo itself was mounted low down on the right side of the engine and pushed air through an intercooler mounted alongside the radiator, before the charge was fed to the engine itself. As on the 2002 a KKK turbocharger was used, with maximum boost set at 8.6 psi/0.6 Bar. The normally aspirated 732i produced 197bhp, but the turbocharged unit produced 252bhp – this was an increase of 'only' 28 per cent, as the whole image of the car was intended to be 'executive' rather than 'super sports'.

The 'executive' image was enhanced by the offering of ZF automatic transmission as well as a five-speed manual transmission, and by the ABS anti-lock braking system fitted as standard equipment. Although the first generation 745is were rather obviously turbocharged, a rework of all the electronic engine management systems from 1982 saw the car become even more smooth and sophisticated, without losing any of its formidable performance.

Demand was quite limited, with only about 2,500 to 3,000 745is being built every year.

The BMW 745i of 1980-1986 shared its spacious five-seater body shell with every other 7-Series saloon. Its engine, though, produced 252bhp and the top speed was in the region of 137mph. It was an exclusive BMW, for only 2,500 to 3,000 745is were built every year.

LEFT From every angle, the 745i was sleek, plump, and somehow self-satisfied. Some commented rather unkindly that this was typical of the burghers of Munich, the city where the car was assembled . . .

BELOW, FAR LEFT In BMW language, 745i should mean that this 7-Series car had a 4.5-litre engine; in reality it was a 3.5-litre unit, with turbocharging to boost the effective capacity.

BELOW LEFT With all this instrumentation in the centre console, the 745i owner could never complain of being ignored. Apart from the radio, there was the complex computer, and driver control over the action of the automatic transmission.

ABOVE RIGHT Even for such a large car, the 745i's engine bay was well filled. The six-cylinder engine had an aluminium cylinder head, and the turbocharger was on the right side of the cylinder block, feeding air across the top of the engine to the inlet manifold.

RIGHT The 745i's engine was large, but extremely well packaged. The air cleaner was ahead of the turbocharger, the air-air intercooler close beside it. At 252bhp, it was a conservatively-rated unit.

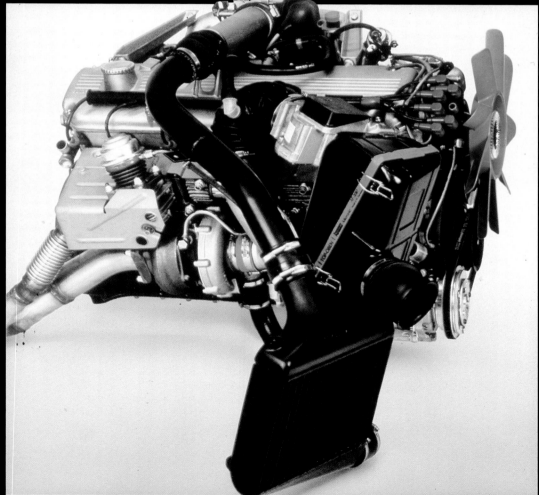

CHEVROLET CORVAIR MONZA SPYDER

PRODUCTION SPAN
1962 and 1964
-
ENGINE
Flat 6 cyl, ohv
-
CAPACITY
145 CID/2.38 litre
-
MAXIMUM POWER
150bhp
-
CHASSIS/SUSPENSION
Unit-construction steel
body/chassis structure,
coil spring/wishbone ifs,
coil spring/semi-trailing
arm irs
-
BODY STYLE
2 door 4 seater
convertible
-
TOP SPEED
100mph/160kph
-
0-60MPH
10.0 seconds
-

In the late 1950s each of North America's 'Big Three' – General Motors, Ford, and Chrysler – designed a smaller and cheaper type of car, for the 'compact' category. Those from Ford and Chrysler were strictly conventional but the GM design, the Chevrolet Corvair, was technically adventurous.

By any previous North American standards the Corvair was different, for GM's designers had obviously been studying the VW 'Beetle' phenomenon. Not only did the Corvair have a rear-mounted engine, but this was an air-cooled unit with a flat-six layout. Because of this the Corvair had a preponderance of weight in the tail, and strong oversteering tendencies. The motoring press greeted the new car with both incredulity and interest, and it went on to have a controversial and stormy career.

The basic style of the Corvair was what became known as the 'inverted bathtub'; there was a pronounced crease all around the waist of the various body styles. Most Corvairs had saloon, estate, or sometimes coupé versions of this style, all on the same 108in/274cm wheelbase . But from the autumn of 1961 a more powerful version known as the 'Monza', sold either as a coupé, or the even more graceful Spyder was put on sale. A turbocharged version of the Spyder – the world's first passenger car application – went on sale in 1962.

This pioneering turbo installation had the turbocharger itself drawing fuel-air mixture through a single carburettor; not, as in modern designs, pushing compressed air into the carburettor or fuel injection system, and the inlet manifold was a relatively crude shape. It was not a very refined installation, but it was important as a pioneer. The Spyder, even though at first it only sold at the rate of 10,000 a year, soon developed a cult all of its own, particularly when powered by the turbocharged engine. The engine, like others with a similar configuration, had a very distinctive exhaust note which added to the character.

Monza Spyders were considerably faster than other Corvairs, had multi-instrument facia panels and a number of other sports and handling accessories all built in to the standard specificaton, and they were certainly more spacious than the alternative imported sports cars of the period.

The two factors militating against the Monza Spyder were cost – $500 extra, nearly a quarter more than that of a normal-engined Coupé – and quirky, somewhat 'nervous', handling. At this time the Corvair was under attack from the consumers' friend, Ralph Nader, and there is no doubt that the adverse publicity harmed sales, even though the Spyder was not an evil handling car at all.

The Monza of this period had very similar 'family' styling to other and larger Chevrolets, but it was a much less decorated car than its larger relatives. Because Corvair sales in general were sliding at this time the turbocharged Monza Spyder was not the success that it might have been, so when the completely re-engineered 1965 Corvair appeared the turbocharged engine was dropped.

RIGHT In 1962 the Corvair Monza Spyder was the world's first turbocharged car to go on general sale. The flat-six engine was air-cooled, and mounted in the tail. The Spyder, by definition, was an open-top car, though other Corvairs were saloons and estate cars.

MIDDLE RIGHT Clearly the idea of a turbocharged engine was ahead of its time: in 1965, the Monza Spyder was dropped from the Corvair range.

BOTTOM RIGHT The Spyder was much more attractive than the more mundane Corvair saloon. It is difficult to tell that this is a rear-engined design, the proportions look so right.

CHRYSLER MASERATI

PRODUCTION SPAN
Introduced 1986

ENGINE
4 cyl, ohc/Twin ohc

CAPACITY
135 CID/2,213cc

MAXIMUM POWER
174/205bhp

CHASSIS/SUSPENSION
Unit-construction steel
body/chassis structure,
coil spring/Macpherson
struts ifs, coil spring
and radius arm rear beam

BODY STYLE
2 door 2+2 seater
convertible

TOP SPEED
124/137mph : 198/219kph

0-60MPH
Not recorded

The industrial scene can sometimes change rapidly. In the late 1970s Chrysler and Maserati were both in major financial difficulties, yet by the mid-1980s both were healthy and active once again. Better still – the two companies had joined forces to produce a new and luxurious car, the Chrysler-Maserati.

The link-up was originally a personal one, for Chrysler's boss Lee Iacocca and Maserati's owner Alejandro DeTomaso had first done business together when Iacocca was at Ford, on the DeTomaso Pantera project. Once Iacocca and his team had rescued Chrysler from oblivion it was natural that a similar image-building project should be considered.

The Chrysler-Maserati was a car designed in Detroit – mechanically and in its styling – while Maserati were charged with the design of the interior and were also responsible for assembly of the production car. The basis of the design was Chrysler's familiar transverse engine/transmission front-wheel-drive package, as used in models like the Le Baron and New Yorker family cars, this time mounted in a specially designed steel monocoque with a 93in/236cm wheelbase.

The new car, which was clearly aimed at the Mercedes-Benz SL market, was a smoothly detailed two-door convertible with 2+2 seating. Like all the latest wind-cheating styles this was a very integrated shape, with wrap-around headlamp/turn-indicator units and a small grille in the nose, matched by a full-width, but slim, display of lamps at the rear. The body was surprisingly long, at 176in/447cm, for a car with such a compact wheelbase, but this ensured a very large boot, even if there was not enough space for four seats. Maserati had tackled the interior style, which featured soft-tuck leather, and a very 'European' ambience.

Each Chrysler-Maserati was to be sold as a full convertible with power-operated soft-top, along with the provision of a lift-off hardtop. The soft top was beautifully tailored, while the smooth hardtop featured portholes in the rear quarters of the type once seen in two-seater Thunderbirds and in other American cars of the 1970s.

The car's engine was not, as some had hoped, from Maserati but was a developed version of Chrysler's own 135 CID/2.2 litre unit, which dated from the 1970s and was specially packaged with front-wheel-drive in mind. For the 'Maserati' there were two versions, both with turbocharging. The 'basic' 174bhp unit was a development of that already being used in Chrysler's other front-drive cars, notably the Chrysler Laser Turbo and Dodge Daytona Turbo cars announced a few years earlier, and originally rated at 146bhp. The more powerful unit had a De Tomaso-developed 16-valve cylinder head and twin overhead camshafts, and produced no less than 205bhp. Without doubt this was the most exciting Chrysler engine for many years. Five-speed manual, or three-speed automatic transmissions were available. Both units used Garrett turbos and air/air intercoolers.

In the late 1980s the category which this car was to contest was becoming positively overcrowded, for the Cadillac Allanté and the latest Mercedes-Benz models were all trying to attract the same customers.

RIGHT When he was at Ford-USA, Lee Iacocca liked doing business with Italian concerns, and in the late 1980s he repeated the trick at Chrysler. The Chrysler Maserati used an American four-cylinder engine, with turbocharging and a choice of cylinder head designs. Exterior styling was American, but Maserati was responsible for the interior style and the assembly of the entire car.

BELOW RIGHT The low nose and high tail are practically *de rigueur* for a mid-eighties car in this class.

CITROEN CX25 GTI TURBO

PRODUCTION SPAN
Introduced 1984

—

ENGINE
4 cyl, ohv

—

CAPACITY
153 CID/2,500cc

—

MAXIMUM POWER
168bhp

—

CHASSIS/SUSPENSION
Unit-construction steel
body/chassis structure,
with subframes, hydro-
pneumatic units/wishbone
ifs, hydro-pneumatic
units and trailing arm
irs, with self-levelling

—

BODY STYLE
4 door 5 seater saloon

—

TOP SPEED
126mph/202kph

—

0–60MPH
8.6 seconds

—

Citroen's finances suffered badly in the early 1970s, but the company pressed ahead with the development of a new car, and announced the large front-drive CX model in 1974. In the next ten years, after being taken over and coming under firm Peugeot control, Citroen produced more and more derivatives of the same basic design, with several engines eventually being used. The powerful petrol-powered turbocharged version finally appeared in 1984, to become the company's high-performance flagship.

As one might have expected from Citroen the CX model was a sleek and technically advanced car, built on a lengthy (112.2in/285cm) wheelbase. Like its predecessor, the DS19/21/23 series, it had front-wheel-drive, all independent self-levelling hydro-pneumatic suspension, power steering and power (disc) brakes. Unlike the DS however the CX's engine was transversely mounted, and the body style was even more wind-cheating than before. Big Citroens seemed to be at their best when making long journeys on fast roads, but they began to feel ungainly on tight and twisty going.

Turbocharging was certain to improve the car's performance, and – at most engine speeds – make it a more responsive machine. Although several more advanced engines were available in the Peugeot-Citroen group by the early 1980s, the old style overhead-valve Citroen unit was retained for conversion into a turbocharged unit. This five-bearing engine had been introduced as a 121 CID/2.0 litre unit in 1965, and had gradually been enlarged to a full 153 CID/2.5 litre size by the late 1970s. All engines of this type used cast iron cylinder blocks, and light-alloy heads.

Because the engine was transversely mounted in the chassis, and featured cross flow breathing, the Garrett turbocharger could easily be installed alongside the block, at the front of the car, ideally placed for being kept cool. Compared with the normally-aspirated GTi, the compression ratio was reduced from 8:75:1 to 7:75:1, but the power peak rose from 138bhp to 168bhp; maximum boost pressure was 8 psi/0.55 Bar. As with the normal GTi, Bosch L-Jetronic fuel injection was used.

The rather limited power output – 67.2bhp/litre was developed – was partly due to the old design of the engine itself, partly due to a decision to go for good low-speed response and flexibility, and partly because no intercooler was fitted. One look inside the crowded engine bay shows that there could have been little space for one to be installed – and the inlet passages would have been even more convoluted if an intercooler had been included.

To match the chassis to the new-found power, the CX was given much wider wheels, and there was a sleek spoiler mounted in the hatchback lid. There was, however, no way that so much power and torque could be fed through the front wheels without any wheelspin developing – which was actually embarrassingly present during fast acceleration from rest, or in very wet weather. Like all such CXs, the GTi Turbo was a strong, under steering car.

RIGHT Citroen's CX range was very advanced when launched in 1974, and still modern in outlook in the late 1980s. The turbocharged version was put on sale in 1984, its 168bhp being kept under control by revised suspension, wider wheels, and slight changes to the aerodynamics. There was a face-lift to the nose on the Turbo 2, which modernized the mid-1970s styling.

BELOW RIGHT This stylized letter 'T' was Citroen's was of telling the world that *this* model had turbocharging.

BELOW, FAR RIGHT Citroen's approach to air-smoothing was always thorough. On the CX Turbo there was not only a transverse spoiler, but a concave-shaped rear window and part-covers over the rear wheels. The suspension was self-levelling, to suit all loading conditions.

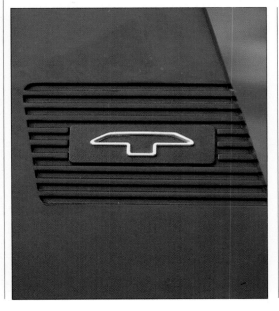

DODGE DAYTONA TURBO

PRODUCTION SPAN
Introduced 1983

ENGINE
4 cyl, ohc

CAPACITY
153 CID/2,213cc

MAXIMUM POWER
146/174bhp

CHASSIS/SUSPENSION
Unit-construction steel
body/chassis structure,
coil spring/Macpherson
strut ifs, coil spring
and radius arm beam

BODY STYLE
2 door 4 seater coupé

TOP SPEED
125/137mph : 200/219kph

0-60MPH
Not recorded

Dodge is one of several marques used by the Chrysler Corporation, the smallest of Detroit's 'Big Three' in the USA. By 1978, when that flamboyant personality Lee Iacocca joined the company from Ford, Chrysler's finances were in terrible shape. It was a modern industrial miracle that Iacocca's team not only turned the company round, but saw a number of fast-selling new cars developed; by the late 1980s Chrysler was very profitable indeed.

The secret of the rebirth was the 'K-Car', a completely new front-wheel-drive chassis, with transversely-mounted engine, that was under development when Iacocca arrived. The first K-Cars, conventional saloons and estate cars such as the Dodge Aries, were launched in the autumn of 1980, and in the years which followed a whole series of new body styles were added on the same basic platform. Two of them were the fast coupé twins – Chrysler Laser and Dodge Daytona.

The secret of the K-Cars was not only their front-wheel-drive, and their small size (they were about 900lb/408kg lighter than the old rear-drive cars they replaced), but the fact that they had a brand new engine, the first introduced at Chrysler for 21 years.

Specifically laid out for transverse installation, and for the economy-conscious 1980s, the new unit was a 135 CID/2,213cc four-cylinder design, complete with overhead camshaft valve gear and hydraulic tappets. In 1981-model guise the engine developed a mere 84bhp but there was a lot of potential locked inside, ready for exploitation in the faster and more sporty coupés. Early saloons had four-speed transmission but a five-speeder was on the way, and a three-speed automatic was also available.

The sporty 'twins' – Laser and Daytona – were launched in the autumn of 1973, both on the same 97in/246.5cm wheelbase as the later K-Car saloons, with the same glassback styling but with different noses and other details. 'Base' cars had fuel-injection, normal aspiration and 99bhp, but there was also a Garrett-turbocharged version of the engine with 146bhp. The Chrysler 'Laser' was a new model name but the alternative 'Dodge Daytona' revived strong memories of previous and much larger Dodges of the 1960s and 1970s.

Right away the higher powered versions provided real competition for rivals such as the Ford Mustang III and the smaller engined versions of the Chevrolet Camaro. Along with the K-Car saloons and their derivatives this all helped to bring Chrysler back into a healthy position.

Then, for 1986 and 1987, the corporation announced the next evolution of this design. For 1986 an enlarged 153 CID/2.5 litre version of the normally aspirated engine became available. For 1987, although the Chrysler Laser version was dropped completely, the Dodge Daytona was restyled with a smoother and more wind-cheating nose, and given a new version of the original 135 CID/2.2 litre engine complete with intercooler, which developed no less than 174bhp, and made the latest Daytona a very fast car indeed.

It was on this excellent modern chassis that the specialized Chrysler-Maserati was also developed.

RIGHT The Dodge Daytona Turbo was launched in 1983, and so well that it was still being made in essentially the same form in 1988. The layout featured a transversely-mounted front engine, and front-wheel-drive. Headlamps were normally hidden away. This was the 'chassis' from which the flamboyant Chrysler-Maserati was developed.

BELOW RIGHT Like other European cars of the same size and performance category, the Daytona Turbo had a smoothly cut-off tail, a small spoiler, and a lift-up hatchback.

FERRARI F1

PRODUCTION SPAN
Introduced 1981
—
ENGINE
V6 cyl, Twin ohc
—
CAPACITY
91.5 CID/1,496cc
—
MAXIMUM POWER
560bhp in 1981, rising
to 880/900bhp in 1986
—
CHASSIS/SUSPENSION
Aluminium honeycomb
and carbon fibre
composite chassis/body
structure, coil spring and
wishbone ifs, coil spring
and wishbone irs
—
BODY STYLE
Single-seater F1 car
—
TOP SPEED
Never recorded
—
0-60MPH
Never recorded
—

When a new formula was introduced for Grand Prix racing in 1966 it specified two types of engine – normally-aspirated 183 CID/3 litre types, or 91.5 CID/1.5 litre 'supercharged' units, with normal road-car fuel to be used. At the time most designers agreed that the normally aspirated engines would be most powerful, so no supercharged engines were developed. For many years therefore the dominant engines were the V8 Cosworth DFV and the flat-12 Ferrari units; by the early 1980s both types were producing about 520bhp.

This period predated the building of practical turbocharged engines. Once Porsche had shown that turbocharged racing units could not only be very powerful, but reliable over long distances, Formula 1 designers began to look at similar engines for their single seater race cars.

The F1 pioneer was Renault whose turbocharged V6 first raced in 1977 (and first won in 1979); but next to come along, and most significant, was Ferrari. Throughout the 1970s, Ferrari had used a normally aspirated flat 12 engine, which won many races, but by 1980 it had reached its limit.

Ing Forghieri's team then designed a 91.5 CID/1.5 litre turbocharged unit, the company's first. This was unveiled in 1980, started its first race in 1981, and won for the first time at Monaco in 1981. The Ferrari team went on to win the Constructors' Championship in 1982 and by 1983 most other teams had switched to turbocharged engines. Before long the normally aspirated engines were completely outclassed.

Except that most F1 cars changed over from using light-alloy monocoques to using carbon fibre and other technically advanced materials, the main technological advance during the mid and late 1980s was in the power developed by the engines. Between 1966 and 1980 normally-aspirated engines improved gradually from 400bhp to 520bhp. Between 1977 and 1986 (when fuel consumption regulations began to bite) the best turbocharged power outputs rocketed from 550bhp to 900bhp in 'race trim' – and perhaps up to 1,200bhp in 'qualifying' trim!

Ferrari's engine was typical of this. It started life in 1981 as a light-alloy 120-degree 91.5 CID/1.5 litre V6 unit, with twin overhead-camshafts and four valves per cylinder. In early months two different types of forced induction – turbocharging, and Comprex BBC pressure-wave supercharging – were tested, but the turbo soon reigned supreme.

RIGHT By the end of 1987 Ferrari was back on top, winning races with its turbocharged F1 car. This is the Australian GP, won by the Austrian driver Gerhard Berger.

BELOW LEFT All the glamour of Ferrari in F1 racing – the Portuguese GP 1987. Michele Alboreto at the wheel, in this pit shot, with 900 bhp of turbocharged engine behind his head, ready for action.

ABOVE In 1982 Ferrari's F1 engine was a 120-degree V6 unit, with twin turbos mounted above the engine, and with short exhaust megaphones attached direct to them. At that time, peak power was 'only' 580 bhp.

The 1981 engine had exhaust ports in the centre of the 'V', which meant that twin KKK turbochargers could be mounted above the main castings, with short exhaust pipes pointing straight out to the tail. Massive intercoolers were positioned one each side of the chassis tub, and in this form the engine produced about 560bhp at 11,000rpm.

The power increased steadily in the years which followed – to 580bhp in 1982, 620bhp in 1983, and 680bhp in 1984. For 1985 there was a major redesign, with new cylinder heads and exhaust ports on the outside of the engine. This allowed the twin KKK turbos to be mounted low down, at each side of the tub, where they were more easily cooled than before. For 1985 Ferrari claimed 780bhp, and during 1986 up to 880bhp was used; at times, with short-life 'qualifying boost' the unit produced up to 1,000bhp – all these figures being typical of the horsepower levels used by other F1 engines at the time. Such outputs could only be reached by using huge boost figures – up to 57.6 psi/4 Bar in 1986.

F1 engines of this period, were the most efficient turbocharged motor car units ever devised, for they could be expected to race with up to 600bhp/litre, and to be reliable for flat out use for two hours. Most engine failures, when they occurred, were caused by turbo failure, usually because of a breakdown in lubrication to the shafts.

The rules obliged F1 cars to run with much reduced boost in 1988, and they would be banned altogether for 1989.

FERRARI GTO

PRODUCTION SPAN
1984 to 1987

ENGINE
V8 cyl, Twin ohc

CAPACITY
174 CID/2,855cc

MAXIMUM POWER
400bhp

CHASSIS/SUSPENSION
Separate steel chassis structure, steel and composite body shell, coil spring and wishbone ifs, coil spring and wishbone irs

BODY STYLE
2 door 2 seater coupé

TOP SPEED
188mph/301kph

0-60MPH
4.8 seconds

The charismatic initials 'GTO' mean, in Italian, 'Gran Turismo Omologato', which indicates that the car has been built in sufficient numbers for it to be approved for motorsport use. The original Ferrari GTO was a front-engined V12 three litre, produced between 1962 and 1964, but the 1980s variety was at once faster, more sophisticated and more numerous.

The story really began with the Dino 246GT of 1969–73, which had a neat and rigid chassis and a transversely-mounted V8 engine. This gave way to the 308GTB of 1975, which had a 17 CID/2.9 litre 90-degree four-cam V8 engine, and absolutely unmistakeable Pininfarina styling.

The GTO, which was launched at the Geneva Motor Show in March 1984, was loosely based on the 308GTB but was much more powerful and better in many other respects. In spite of the fashionable trends towards four-wheel-drive and anti-lock brakes, the GTO had neither feature – what it had, in huge quantities, was performance, charisma, and breeding. At the time Ferrari said it would only build 200 examples, the minimum required to gain (sporting) Group B approval, but in the end 271 cars were produced, the last of all being delivered to Niki Lauda early in 1987.

At one time the plan had been for the GTO to be raced and used in high-speed tarmac rallies, but nothing came of either scheme. So the GTO became a supreme road car or a glorious collector's piece for future generations to admire.

Compared with the 308GTB/328GTB the GTO had a lengthened wheelbase but very similar chassis engineering and styling. The engine was no longer mounted athwartships, but was positioned longitudinally in the classic sports-racing position, with a new five-speed transmission/transaxle behind it.

To bring the effective engine capacity within the 244 CID/4 litre class limit (for the turbo 'factor' of 1.4:1 had to be applied), the V8 engine's capacity was slightly reduced, from 178 CID/2,926cc to 174 CID/2,855cc and was equipped with two Japanese IHI turbochargers, one to each bank. Naturally, a pair of intercoolers were also fitted and the result was peak power of 400bhp, developed at 7,000rpm.

The body shell of the 'ordinary' GTO (as opposed to the 'Evolution' GTO which Ferrari once threatened to produce but never actually built in numbers) was mainly in steel, but a number of plastics and even honeycomb composite materials were also used.

Here was a car for the connoisseur, a car likely to be outpaced by only one or two other models ever built. On the rare occasions when a GTO's performance was measured, it was seen to have a top speed of nearly 190mph, flashing acceleration and quite peerless steering, handling and general agility. It was the nearest thing to a true racing car that anyone was ever likely to be able to drive on the road.

Could it ever be bettered? Ferrari thought so – the result being the launch of the F40 model in 1987, to celebrate the company's fortieth birthday in the automobile business.

Ferrari's 1980s-style GTO was a limited-edition car originally developed with Group B competition in mind. The engine was a twin turbocharged V8 unit offering 400 bhp in 'standard' form. Styling, as ever with such Ferraris, was by Pininfarina. The sculpted section along the doors (below) led to intakes in the flanks, to feed air to the mid-mounted engine.

FIAT 124 SPIDER TURBO

PRODUCTION SPAN
1981 and 1982

ENGINE
4 cyl, Twin ohc

CAPACITY
122 CID/1,995cc

MAXIMUM POWER
120bhp

CHASSIS/SUSPENSION
Steel unit-construction
body/chassis structure,
coil spring and wishbone
ifs, coil spring and
radius arm rear beam

BODY STYLE
2 door 2+2 seater
sports car

TOP SPEED
110mph/176kph

0-60MPH
9.2 seconds

Fiat was still relatively inexperienced in the sports car business when it launched the 124 Sport Spider in 1966, but this car soon became very popular indeed. Over the years the specification gradually improved and in 1982 the entire project was handed over to Pininfarina for its final few years.

The Spider's structure was a pressed steel monocoque by Pininfarina, built up on the basis of a shortened 124 saloon platform with beam axle rear suspension and worm-and-roller steering. The style was neat and quite unmistakeable; rather like the British MGB, it made the transition from 1960s to 1980s without ever seeming to be out of date.

The secret of the 124 Spider's appeal was its engine, a brand new four cylinder twin-overhead camshaft design intended for mass production and for fitment to many different cars. This Fiat design is now seen as a classic in every way, for hundreds of thousands were still being made every year of the late 1980s, and examples were found not only in sports cars and coupés but in front-wheel-drive hatchbacks, rear-drive saloons and in four-wheel-drive rally specials.

Originally the Spider's engine was an 85 CID/1.4 litre unit, developing 90bhp, but by 1978 it had been enlarged, redesigned and refined into a long-stroke 122 CID/2.0 litre size. This had been done to keep it abreast of burgeoning USA exhaust emission regulations, for cleaning up the emissions also tended to involve de-tuning the engine as well.

Tuned for the European market, the 122 CID/1,995cc engine could produce more than 122bhp, but in USA de-toxed guise it was strangled back to a mere 87bhp which was even less than the original 124 Sport Spider had boasted in 1966. It was to rectify this shortfall in performance in North America that Fiat-USA decided to sponsor its own turbocharged engine conversion, and to back it with its own warranty.

The Spider 2,000's engine was worked over by Fred Dellis of Legend Industries, who just happened to be a Fiat dealer as well. It was a simple conversion, naturally using a Garrett AiResearch turbocharger but no intercooler; the Bosch L-Jetronic injection, newly standardized on normally aspirated 124 Spiders sold in the USA, was retained. Sales began in 1981.

The improvement was worth having, for peak power was improved from 103bhp to 120bhp, and peak torque went up from 112lbft to 130lbft. As far as the customer was concerned it converted the Fiat Spider from a rather lumbering machine which struggled to reach 100mph to a more spritely machine which could top 110mph in favourable circumstances.

All 124s of this type handled well without being outstanding in any way, and had neat but by no means flamboyant styling. Hundreds of thousands of these cars were sold from 1966 to 1986, when assembly of Pininfarina models finally ceased, but less than a thousand had the USA-only turbocharger conversion, which was dropped at the end of 1982.

RIGHT Pininfarina styled the Fiat 124 Spider in the mid-1960s, but it still looked smart in the early 1980s. The turbocharged version was sold only in the USA, in 1981 and 1982. Later this car was rebadged as a Pininfarina model, instead of a Fiat.

FAR RIGHT Like the MG MGB, the 124 Spider style looked good when new, and elegant when old. Except that this car has Pininfarina badges on the nose, it was identical to early 1980s Fiats. The twin 'power bulges' in the bonnet pressing are for effect, not for function.

BELOW RIGHT As sold for the USA markets, the Fiat 124 Spider had a compact and neatly detailed nose. It is hard to see that those are energy-absorbing bumpers.

FORD ESCORT RS TURBO

PRODUCTION SPAN
Introduced 1985
—
ENGINE
4 cyl, ohc
—
CAPACITY
97.5 CID/1,597cc
—
MAXIMUM POWER
132bhp
—
CHASSIS/SUSPENSION
Unit-construction steel body/chassis structure, coil spring/Macpherson strut ifs, coil springs and multi-link irs
—
BODY STYLE
2 door 4 seater saloon
—
TOP SPEED
125mph/200kph
—
0–60MPH
8.1 seconds
—

Ford introduced the first range of Escort saloons in 1968, revised the car in 1975, but did not produce a front-wheel-drive Escort (the Mk 3) until the autumn of 1980. This was a car which was to be built in several European countries, with a rather different (but obviously related) Escort also being built in the USA. By the late 1980s Escorts of all types were the fastest selling cars in the world.

The European Escort Mk 3 was designed around a range of new and transversely mounted overhead-camshaft engines. At first the most powerful model was a carburetted 97.5 CID/1.6 litre version (XR3) which produced 96bhp, but two years later this unit was given fuel injection (XR3i) and produced 105bhp. At the same time a 115 bhp RS1600i (with injection) was put on sale, a turbocharged conversion kit was produced for the carburetted cars, and this was used in a British one-make rally championship series. Such rallies, in which only one make (and sometimes only one model of one make) is eligible, are a cheap way of providing motor sport, and a method of encouraging the latent driving talent of those who cannot get their hands on a superior car.

At the end of 1984 a new Escort RS Turbo was launched. It was the amalgam of several previous derivatives and aimed at motor sport usage. This car looked like the XR3i but had extended wheel arches and door sills, it used RS1600i suspension components and wheels and with turbocharging allied to fuel injection it produced 132bhp; like almost all other Mk3 models the engine retained hydraulic tappets. In the package was Bosch KE-Jetronic injection, a Garrett T3 turbocharger, and a complex but efficient electronic engine management system.

It was the first 'own-design' turbocharged engine ever put on the market by Ford of Europe, for the contemporary Merkur XR4Ti used a Ford-USA engine originally developed for use in the Mustang III.

Ford said it would build only 5,000 such cars – all painted white – but eventually sold nearly double that number. In 1986 a less obviously sporting, 'Mk 3½' RS Turbo took over as the top-of-the-range Escort model; this had softer suspension, higher gearing and mechanical anti-lock braking.

The turbocharged engine was a developed version of the original conversion kit and had the turbocharger mounted low down at the side (or front as installed in the car) of the block. An air-to-air intercooler was fixed behind the car's front grille, and in competition form the engine could be boosted to double its standard output.

To keep all this performance in check the Escort RS Turbo was fitted with a viscous coupling limited-slip differential – it was the world's first front-drive car to have such a component – firm suspension, wide rim wheels and fat tyres. It looked, felt and behaved like a real production racer.

Ford, like Saab before it, designed this turbocharged installation to give good pulling power from moderate engine revs, but the unit was still pulling strongly when it reached the limit of 6,200rpm in intermediate gears. It was typical of the modern generation of turbocharged units, neither too peaky nor too temperamental, yet a lot more torquey than its normally aspirated version.

RIGHT Ford's Escort RS Turbo shared its body structure and front engine/front-wheel-drive layout with the Escort XR3i. The turbocharged engine, however, gave it a top speed of 125mph, and there was a limited-slip differential to keep the power in check. This is the facelifted version introduced in 1986.

MIDDLE RIGHT This front view of the Escort RS Turbo's transversely-mounted engine shows the turbocharger mounted ahead of the unit, immediately behind the car's nose, with the intercooler alongside it.

BELOW RIGHT Unlike the XR3i, the Escort RS Turbo had cooling louvres in the bonnet and styling sills under the doors. The cast alloy wheels were standard, as was the 125mph performance!

FORD CAPRI

2.8 TURBO

PRODUCTION SPAN
1981 and 1982
-
ENGINE
V6 cyl, ohv
-
CAPACITY
170 CID/2,792cc
-
MAXIMUM POWER
188bhp
-
CHASSIS/SUSPENSION
Unit-construction steel
body/chassis structure,
coil spring/Macpherson
strut ifs, half elliptic
spring rear beam
-
BODY STYLE
2 door 4 seater saloon
-
TOP SPEED
135mph/216kph
-
0-60MPH
8.0 seconds
-

The first Capris were put on sale in 1969, following the same marketing approach as the Ford Mustang of the USA. The cars had sharply styled coupé bodywork and a cramped four seater cabin with a wide variety of engines. The fastest and most exciting Capris were always those powered by V6 engines.

From 1974 the Capris became Mk II, with smoother styling and a hatchback feature, while from 1978 this was facelifted to become Mk III, with a four-headlamp nose and enhanced equipment. This was the car for which a factory developed turbo-conversion was made available during 1981 and 1986.

In the 1970s much modified Capris had been extremely successful in saloon and prototype racing categories, with the West German Zakspeed concern building the fastest and fiercest cars of all. It was to celebrate the success of the Zakspeed cars that Ford produced a mere 200 turbocharged cars for sale in West Germany.

For many years two completely different types of V6 engine were fitted to Capris, the British 183 CID/3 litre, and the West German 170 CID/2.8 litre, the turbocharging conversion was carried out on the 170 CID/2.8 litre unit, which was about to become the 'favoured' V6 throughout Ford of Europe.

In normally aspirated form, a 2.8 with Weber carburation produced 135bhp, and with Bosch fuel injection it produced 160bhp. The injected type had already been chosen for use in the forthcoming 2.8i, yet when Zakspeed tackled the Capri Turbo it was decided to base this on the less powerful Weber-carburetted version! Illogical? Maybe, but from time to time large car companies are like that.

Zakspeed did not want to overreach themselves nor make the Capri's brakes work too hard, so the single KKK turbocharger was set to give a maximum boost of 5.5psi/0.38 Bar; as a result the power output was limited to 188bhp, only 28bhp more than the normally aspirated 2.8i, but sufficient to give the car a top speed of around 135mph/216kph. The suspension, handling and stability were the same as those of other large-engined Capris.

Because it was separately developed from the popular 2.8i model (a UK enterprise even though built in West Germany), the 2.8T had its own unique features. The wheels were the four spoke alloys already well known as Ford's 'RS' type, there was a big new spoiler under the front bumper, a bigger and unique tailgate spoiler and flared wheel arches. Body modifications were carried out by Zakspeed but final assembly was in Cologne.

Some 2.8Ts had solid front disc brakes but later cars used the ventilated discs of the 2.8i. All cars had the beefy four speed transmission and a limited-slip differential was optional.

This factory sponsored turbo-Capri should not be confused with the Aston Martin Tickford Capri which had more stylish and more extensive body modifications, and a fuel-injected engine complete with IHI turbocharger and 205bhp power output. 100 of these cars were produced between 1984 and 1987, many fewer than AMT originally forecast.

Ford's limited-edition Capri 2.8 Turbo had a 2.3-litre V6 turbocharged engine producing 188 bhp. Surprisingly, this was not achieved with fuel injection, but with the help of a Weber carburettor.

BELOW RIGHT The interior is somewhat cramped and spartan but functional. This is the 1981 model.

The high-mounted rear wing was functional (above), as was the deep front spoiler (left), and there was nothing modest about the car's badging.

FORD SIERRA
RS COSWORTH

PRODUCTION SPAN
1986 and 1987
-
ENGINE
4 cyl, twin ohc
-
CAPACITY
122 CID/1,993cc
-
MAXIMUM POWER
204/224bhp
-
CHASSIS/SUSPENSION
Unit-construction steel
body/chassis structure,
coil spring/Macpherson
strut ifs, coil spring
and semi-trailing
arm irs
-
BODY STYLE
2 door 4 seater saloon
hatchback
-
TOP SPEED
145mph/232kph
-
0-60MPH
6.2 seconds
-

The very name of this car summarizes its ancestry, and its purpose. The Sierra was Ford's smoothly styled mid-sized hatchback for the 1980s, RS means 'Rally Sport', and Cosworth denotes the name of the famous UK designer of competition engines. The Sierra RS Cosworth was, quite simply, a specially developed and limited production machine, built to succeed in motorsport. The car proved to be remarkably competitive, winning more rallies and races in its first season than any previous Ford car.

The new car, which always seems to be called 'Cosworth', was conceived in 1983, put on sale in 1986, and began its motorsport career from 1 January 1987. In essence it used a three door Sierra structure and suspensions, but had a completely new engine and transmission, and the final drive from a larger new Ford, the Granada Scorpio.

Before this car was conceived Cosworth Engineering had already produced a normally aspirated twin-overhead-cam 16 valve conversion for Ford's existing 122 CID/2 litre engine, as a private venture. Ford then asked Cosworth to produce a turbocharged version of the design, chosen for use in the new car.

For installation in the Sierra's engine bay, Cosworth mounted the Garrett AiResearch turbocharger high on the right side of the engine, and the pressurized air was fed forward to an intercooler mounted at the front of the car, close to the water radiator, and then to the inlet manifold on the other side of the car. Weber Marelli fuel injection and electronic engine management systems were also used.

Right from the start the engine was stressed, and all the gas passages shaped, for a competition unit to produce more than 300bhp in race-car trim, but for road use it was considerably de-tuned, and rated at 204bhp. The standard 122 CID/2 litre single-cam Ford engine, by the way, only produced 115bhp in fuel-injected guise.

Engineers in Ford's Special Vehicle Engineering division matched this phenomenal new engine to an American Borg Warner transmission, added larger air intakes at the front and fitted a monstrous spoiler at the rear to produce down force at high speeds, 5,000 examples were built during 1986.

This however was not the end of the turbocharged Cosworth engine. In motorsport terms, what is called an 'evolution' version (the RS500 Cosworth) was then developed, with extra aerodynamic spoilers, and a further modified engine. By fitting a larger Garrett turbocharger – a T31/T04 instead of the familiar T3 – along with a larger intercooler, a double bank of fuel injectors and modified engine internals, the engine's power was boosted to 224 bhp. More important was that for racing purposes this could be improved to no less than 450bhp. 500 of these cars were built in the summer of 1987.

The Sierra RS Cosworth, and especially the RS500 Cosworth version, was an extrovert machine which handled and performed like the de-tuned race car that it was. For 1988 a much more sophisticated version of the 204bhp chassis, using the new four door Sapphire body style, was put on sale.

RIGHT The Sierra RS Cosworth was conceived as a 5,000-off 'homologation special', to allow the car to be used in international motor sport. In that form it had a 204bhp turbocharged Cosworth engine. In mid-1987, Ford (with the help of Aston Martin Tickford) produced a further 500 cars called Sierra RS500 Cosworths, with 224bhp engines, larger intercoolers, more tuning potential, and with modifications to the aerodynamics. The RS500 Cosworth, shown here, had an enlarged engine air intake, and a deeper front spoiler.

LEFT The original Sierra RS Cosworth had one massive rear spoiler, mounted on a pylon on the hatchback panel. For the RS500, depicted here, that spoiler was given a rear lip, and a second spoiler was added below it. Both RS and RS500 models were capable of at least 150mph in standard form. The spoilers really came into their own in touring car racing; the cars won the World Touring Car Championship in 1987.

ABOVE The Cosworth-developed engine of the Sierra features twin overhead camshafts, four valves per cylinder, turbocharging, and Weber-Marelli fuel injection. This was the 500-off RS500 version, with larger turbo, and twin fuel injector rails.

RIGHT Cosworth designed the Sierra RS Cosworth engine around the basis of the T88/'Pinto' type of cylinder block, and manufactured all the engines in its own new factory. In this 'exploded' view, the turbocharger and exhaust manifold has been moved bodily away from the head to show the internal layout, and the belt drive to the camshafts.

OPPOSITE The Sierra RS Cosworth and RS500 Cosworth bodies were like those of mass-market three-door Sierras, but had deeper front spoilers, large rear spoilers, wheel arch extensions, and cooling slots in the bonnet panels.

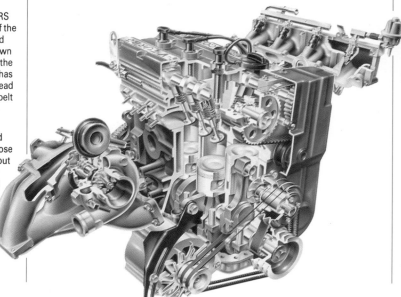

FORD RS200

PRODUCTION SPAN
1985 and 1986

ENGINE
4 cyl, twin ohc

CAPACITY
110 CID/1,803cc

MAXIMUM POWER
250bhp

CHASSIS/SUSPENSION
Steel and composite
body/chassis structure,
double coil spring/
wishbone ifs, double
coil spring and
wishbone irs

BODY STYLE
2 door 2 seater coupé

TOP SPEED
145mph/232kph

0-60MPH
6.1 seconds

As with other fast, specialized and compact turbocharged cars like the Lancia Delta S4 and the Peugeot 205 Turbo 16, Ford's RS200 was developed to compete in the Group B category of rallying. According to the rules, only 200 such cars had to be built to gain approval for use in motorsport, and this was precisely the number produced by Ford.

The project was conceived in 1983, the first car ran in 1984, and the 200 cars were completed in a rented Reliant factory in the Midlands in the winter of 1985 and 1986. Some cars were produced in stripped-out 'rally' trim, some fully equipped for road use, some with left-hand and some with right-hand drive; all were finished in white, the better for a sponsor's colour scheme to be added on top.

The layout was more race car than road car, for advanced composite materials including carbon fibre were used in the structure, the engine was mounted amidships, the main transmission was between the passengers' footwells, and the car had four-wheel drive. The two seater coupé style was by Ghia, and was fashioned from glass-fibre body skin panels; this style included upward facing radiator outlets, and a large rear spoiler so that aerodynamic downforce would be developed as speed rose.

The only Ford 'production car' component in this car was the engine, this being known as the BDT type, which denoted a turbocharged version of the famous Ford-Cosworth BDA engine, a light-alloy four cylinder 16 valve twin-cam design previously used in cars like the Escort RS1600s and Escort RS1800s. In the RS200 it was a 110 CID/1,803cc size, the largest 'BD' so far built in quantity. Because there was plenty of space in the new car's engine bay, the Garrett T03/T04 turbocharger was mounted well clear of the engine on the right side, with ducting leading pressurized air to a roof mounted air-air intercooler, and thence to the Bosch fuel injected inlet manifold on the left side.

In standard '200-off' form the engine was rated at 250bhp – an impressive 139bhp/litre – but for rally use it could be boosted further, to 420bhp at the start of the 1986 season, and to 450bhp by its end. Drive from the engine was taken to a five speed gearbox, and in the transaxle there was originally a choice between 'free' four-wheel-drive, 'locked' four-wheel-drive, or rear-drive only, a complication later dropped from the road cars.

The RS200 was at once small but quite heavy, a pure two seater with very little stowage capacity but magnificent handling combined with a surprisingly supple ride. Like most such 'homologation specials' the RS200 was not an ideal road car, for it was cramped, quite noisy and needed cosseting from cold. Even so, when sales began at the end of 1986, a number of philosophical customers willingly paid their £49,950 (about $82,000 at 1987 prices) for a distinctive car with peerless hand-ling and great personality.

Although the Group B category in rallying was cancelled at the end of 1986, 2.1 litre 'Evolution' versions of the RS200, complete with 600bhp, were successful in 1987 rallycross events.

RIGHT The RS200 was a specially-designed 200-off 'homologation special' with a mid-mounted turbocharged engine, and four-wheel-drive. It was strictly a two seater, with glass-fibre body skins. Standard cars developed 250bhp, but for rallying, up to 450bhp was available, and 2.1-litre versions in rallycross developed 600bhp in 1987 events. An RS200 won the British Rallycross GP in that year.

BELOW RIGHT The RS200 was engineered in the UK, but styled in Italy by Ford's subsidiary, Ghia. It was a stubby little car, with the engine behind the two seats, four- wheel-drive, and with the main gearbox between the driver's and passenger's legs. The scoop in the roof fed the air-air intercooler. Cast alloy wheels were standard, and a few standard Ford Sierra parts (such as screen, glass and steering column) were also used.

ABOVE On the RS200, the whole of the rear bodywork hinged upwards to give access to the engine and the rear suspension. The turbocharger was on the right side of the engine bay, feeding air through the roof-mounted turbocharger, to the inlet manifold on the left. Note that twin spring/damper units are fitted all round.

LEFT The RS200's 1.8-litre engine was dubbed BDT, which stood for Belt Driven (Camshafts), Turbocharged. The 'base' engine was the BDA unit which had been used on several 'hot' Escorts in the 1970s. The derivative shown, the BDT-E, was a high-output 2.1-litre version, for use in the E-for-Evolution model.

RIGHT The RS200 competition car made its World Championship rallying debut in Sweden in February 1986, where it took third place. During the 1986 season, RS200s won 19 International rallies, and in 1987 the cars began winning in rallycross events as well.

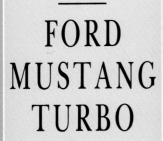

FORD MUSTANG TURBO

PRODUCTION SPAN
1978 and 1986

ENGINE
4 cyl, ohc

CAPACITY
140 CID/2,301cc

MAXIMUM POWER
116/145/175/200bhp

CHASSIS/SUSPENSION
Steel unit-construction
body/chassis structure,
coil spring/wishbone
ifs, coil spring and
radius arm rear beam

BODY STYLE
2 door 4 seater coupé

TOP SPEED
111 to 125mph/178 to
200kph, depending
on engine

0 – 60MPH
Not recorded

RIGHT Ford-USA embraced the philosophy of turbocharged four-cylinder engines in 1978, but for this, the Mustang SVO of 1984, its power was pushed up to 175bhp. The bonnet scoop was meant to direct fresh air to the engine intake.

Ford launched its original Mustang in 1964, this sporty car soon becoming the fastest selling car in the company's history. The original type was replaced by the much smaller Mustang II for 1974, and the third generation car took over in the autumn of 1978.

This, like its predecessors, was a front engine/rear drive car, offered with a bewildering variety of engines – fours, sixes, V6s, and V8s – and for eight years a turbocharged version of overhead-cam 'four' was always available.

Even though American cars were already in the process of being down sized, enthusiasts still loved to drive behind big and rumbly V8s, so this highly-tuned 'four' always had to struggle for its sales.

Except for its engines, the Mustang III was a strictly conventional car, with almost-four-seater coupé bodywork on a 100.6in./255.5cm wheelbase platform. In 1978, when it was new, the lines were rather sharply detailed and angular, but these were gradually softened and modernized over the years.

The four cylinder engine was related in design, but not in detail, to the Ford-Europe 2 litre (as found in Capris, Cortinas and Sierras of the 1970s and 1980s), and was always known as 'Lima' after the first Ford-USA model in which it was used. By the late 1970s it had grown to 140.5 CID/2.4 litres and was used in many different Ford and Lincoln models.

A turbocharged derivative, developing a mere 116bhp at first, was available for the Mustang right from the start, which was further boosted for later model Mustangs and other Ford-Mercury-Lincoln products during the 1980s. In the beginning, the Garrett-turbocharged engine lacked an intercooler, and was no match for the alternative, more torquey, V8 engined Mustangs.

For 1983 it was offered with a redeveloped turbo tune, with more boost, and rated at 145bhp, which gave the car a 120mph top speed. A year later however Ford-USA's new German born motorsport boss, Mike Kranefuss, masterminded the launch of the sporty, red-blooded, Mustang SVO Coupé, which not only had a biplane rear spoiler (rather like that of the contemporary Sierra XR4i) and much more 'European' handling, but it also had an air-air intercooler engine and produced no less than 175bhp. Matched with a five speed manual transmission this produced a real tyre-smoking Mustang. There was still a lazy-revving 301 CID/4.9 litre V8, with 205bhp, maintaining the Mustang lineage.

Just one year later the SVO's turbocharged engine was boosted even more to produce 200bhp, making the ageing car a real match in performance for GM's Camaros and Firebirds, even if it was not as smart or as fashionably equipped. However, even though this matched the Mustang's large V8 engine option, it was apparently not the car the Americans wanted, and was discontinued at the end of the 1986 model year.

Even so, all the development work put in on this engine was not wasted for it was adopted and retained for the larger, more luxurious up-market Thunderbird.

RIGHT The Mustang SV0 had smart and functional light-alloy wheels with fat tyres to help harness all the power.

FORD THUNDERBIRD TURBO COUPE

PRODUCTION SPAN
Introduced in 1982
–

ENGINE
4 cyl, ohc
–

CAPACITY
140.5 CID/2,301cc
–

MAXIMUM POWER
145/152/193bhp
–

CHASSIS/SUSPENSION
Steel unit-construction
body/chassis structure,
coil spring and
MacPherson strut ifs,
coil spring and radius
arm rear beam
–

BODY STYLE
2 door 5 seater coupé
–

TOP SPEED
(193bhp version)
138mph/221kph
–

0-60MPH
(193bhp version)
7.5 seconds
–

The key to the attraction of this smoothly styled, modern North American car is that it was voted Car of the Year by 'Motor Trend' magazine in 1987. By Detroit standards the modern T-Bird was as outstanding as that.

There have been Ford Thunderbirds since the early 1950s, but the character of the cars changed several times over the decades. The originals were two seater sports roadsters but in the 1960s and 1970s the cars became four seaters, grew larger and were more glossily equipped. They were technically similar to the Lincoln Continental and were dubbed 'Personal Cars' by Ford's publicists. Even though some down-sizing took place in the early 1980s the T-Birds were still un-compromisingly square and conventional machines.

For 1983 Ford changed tack completely and all over the world began introducing a series of cars with much smoother and more wind-cheating lines. In Europe the Sierra was typical of this trend, while in the USA there was the middle-sized Tempo – and the sporty new Thunderbird.

The Thunderbird was the Ford-badged version of a trio of new cars which had all been developed around the same chassis and basic style; the other two cars were the Lincoln Mk VII 'lookalike', and the Mercury Cougar (which featured a notchback, rather than fastback, roof style). The Lincoln and Mercury cars however used V6 and V8 engines, the Thunderbird being the only derivative to use a turbocharged four cylinder unit. All had classically simple suspensions, with beam rear axles but also with increasingly sophisticated damper control.

As already mentioned in the Ford Mustang case study the four-cylinder Ford 'Lima' engine had evolved from the earlier 'Pinto' unit, and was a sturdy four cylinder design with single overhead-camshaft valve gear. The original turbocharged derivative had been unveiled as early as 1978, and during the early 1980s this engine was not only made more refined and more reliable but took on considerably more power at the same time.

The 1983 model Thunderbird was also offered with a 231 CID/3.8 litre V6 engine, while for 1984 there was also a 299 CID/4.9 litre V8, but both were normally aspirated, and it was always the turbocharged 'four' (complete with five-speed transmission) which was lightest and most sporting. The original engine, complete with Japanese-type IHI turbo-charger, produced 145bhp, at which rating Ford claimed a top speed of 112mph; but this was made considerably more powerful for 1987 when an air-air intercooler was added.

In the late 1980s form, therefore, the T-Bird's turbocharged engine featured multi-point fuel injection, offered very progressive turbocharger characteristics (for the turbo effect became apparent very smoothly indeed) and had a peak power output of 193bhp. The same model had a restyled and even lower-drag nose than the original 1983 type, and the result was a quite outstanding top speed which no American customer ever dared to authenticate for himself. It was no wonder that the T-Bird was a race winner in Nascar events, and that it became very popular indeed with the customers.

RIGHT There was a time when Europeans thought that all cars designed in Detroit were angular, gaudily detailed, and sloppily sprung, but all that changed in the 1980s. Ford's late-1980s Thunderbird was not only an extremely graceful car, but it had front-wheel-drive, a very powerful (193bhp) turbocharged engine, and a 138mph top speed which no-one dared to prove on American roads.

LEFT A smooth aerodynamic shape, especially around the nose, was all-important in the late 1980s. The Thunderbird's front lamp cluster featured normal and long-range headlamps, plus turn indicators, all without any disturbance of the airflow.

INDY-RACING TURBO CHARGED RACE CAR– LATE 1980s

PRODUCTION SPAN
Cosworth DFX engine
introduced in 1975
–

ENGINE
V8 cyl, Twin ohc
–

CAPACITY
161 CID/2,643cc
–

MAXIMUM POWER
720bhp using
maximum boost of
'48in. Hg' (18.7 PSI/
1.3 Bar). Up to
1,000bhp with higher
Boost ratings.
–

CHASSIS/SUSPENSION
Typical: Aluminium
honeycomb and carbon
fibre composite chassis/
body structure, coil
spring and wishbone
ifs, coil spring and
wishbone irs
–

BODY STYLE
Single seater CART/
USAC race car
–

TOP SPEED
Never recorded
–

0-60MPH
Never recorded
–

For more than 60 years the most important motor race held in the USA has been the Indy 500, which has always been held at the Indianapolis Raceway at the end of May. This is a simple 2½ mile 'oval' – actually two long and two short straights joined by long 90 degree left-hand corners – which demands great courage from the drivers, allied to vast power outputs and rugged reliability from engines. By the 190s qualifying lap speeds exceeded 200mph, the 500-mile race average usually beating 160mph.

Over the years Indy-formula engine regulations have changed several times, but latterly the main categories have been for 256 CID/4.2 litre normally aspirated units, or for 162 CID/2.65 litre forced-induction engines. European companies like Cooper, Lotus and Lola hastened the adoption of mid-engines in the late 1960s, and by the 1980s two chassis manufacturers – Lola and March – supplied the majority of the cars used at Indianapolis.

One four cylinder engine, the legendary Offenhauser unit was used in both forms for many years, but by the mid-1970s it was at the limit of its reliability. At this point the Vel's Parnelli Jones team (which had also been involved in Formula 1 racing) decided to produce a turbocharged version of the famous Cosworth DFV V8 F1 engine, which was built at Northampton in the UK. That was in 1974 – the engine raced for the first time in 1975, and was officially 'adopted' as the DFX by Cosworth in 1976, who built hundreds of such engines in the next decade.

Race victories followed almost at once, the first Indy 500 win coming in 1978. The DFX has been completely dominant at Indianapolis, and in all premier-formula American single-seater events, ever since. As with Formula I, there have been several changes of regulations in that time. In the mid-1970s Indy engines ran with '80 inches of Mercury' of boost, which equals 24psi/1.7 Bar. To reduce speeds and power outputs maximum permissible boost was progressively reduced by the authorities, and by 1980 was eventually standardized at 48in Hg, or 18.7psi/1.3 Bar. Peak power at this rating was originally 600bhp but was eventually raised to around 720bhp, this figure reached at 11,000rpm. At such reduced levels the DFX was so reliable that it usually did 800 to 1,000 racing miles (two or three entire races) without needing a rebuild.

The DFX was a relatively simple short stroke conversion of the 183 CID/3.0 litre DFV engine, still retaining twin overhead camshafts per cylinder bank (gear driven from the crankshaft), with four valves per cylinder. The massive single turbocharger (several different types were used over the years) was mounted behind the engine, driven by exhaust gas from both banks of cylinders, and pushing air direct to the big inlet manifold plenum which was mounted high above the engine itself. There was no intercooler. From that point, incidentally, the race car's exhaust pipe was very short indeed – just a few inches, straight out of the back of the turbocharger casing.

Expert drivers, like Mario Andretti, who have great experience of F1 and Indy race cars quote the DFX as being a 'bit of a beast', for peak torque was developed at 9,500rpm and there was terrific surge of power from about 8,500rpm.

RIGHT By the 1980s all racing cars were mobile billboards. Under the Pennzoil livery this 1984 CART-racing machine was powered by a turbocharged Cosworth DFX engine. Rick Mears is the driver, while Roger Penske was the entrant.

LEFT Cosworth's turbocharged 'Indy' racing engine is a complicated piece of engineering and plumbing, as this show-stand unit proves.

LANCIA DELTA S4

PRODUCTION SPAN
1985 and 1986

ENGINE
4 cyl, Twin ohc

CAPACITY
107 CID/1,759cc

MAXIMUM POWER
250bhp (road car), up
to 500bhp (rally car)

CHASSIS/SUSPENSION
Steel multi-tubular
chassis structure,
GRP/composite body
shell, coil spring and
wishbone ifs, coil
spring and wishbone irs

BODY STYLE
2 door 2 seater saloon

TOP SPEED
(250bhp version)
140mph/224kph

0-60MPH
6.0 seconds

Lancia is the most successful rallying marque in the world. Since the company became involved in top class rallies in the 1960s its engineers (in conjunction with the Abarth subsidiary) have produced a stream of winners. After the Fulvia there was the Ferrari-engined Stratos, the 037 Rally and – from 1985 – the Delta S4.

S4 was the design chosen to meet the challenge of the latest Group B regulations, which allowed a manufacturer to build a mere 200 cars to gain approval and then to produce a further 20, very special, 'evolution' cars for its own 'works team' use. The cars could be, and were, very special indeed.

Whereas Ford (with the RS200 project) chose to build a car which looked entirely special, Lancia's designers produced a new car clothed in a body looking similar to (but not the same as) a mass production Delta Hatchback. Clearly this was done for publicity reasons, and as the S4 was very successful in a very short competition life the strategy was justified.

In the early 1980s Lancia's front-line rally car had been the 037 Rally, a mid-engined rear-drive coupé with supercharging (not turbocharging), but this was soon being seen off by the first generation of four-wheel-drive cars. The Delta S4 was a purpose-built four-wheel drive car, not only intended to replace the 037, but to beat every other known or projected Group B machine.

Its basis was a very sturdy multi-tube chassis frame, with modified 037-type all-independent suspension. The engine was longitudinally mounted behind the seats with the main gearbox ahead of the engine and between the seats, all linked to a transfer gearbox and propeller shafts driving to the front and rear final drive units.

The engine was a completely new competition design – it was not even loosely based on any existing Lancia (or Fiat) unit – and was fascinatingly detailed. Although in some ways it was merely 'state-of-the-art' (four cylinders, twin-overhead camshafts, 16 valves, and a 107 CID/1.76 litres capacity), in others it broke new ground.

Abarth's opinion was that turbocharging was better than supercharging for top end power, but that supercharging was better for low-speed response and mid-range torque. Accordingly the designers took a pragmatic but very brave decision – the new engine would have both types of pressure charge generation! The initial concept, which was only changed in detail as a result of actual competitions experience, was to use a Volumex-type supercharger in series with a KKK turbocharger, but to arrange for a bypass control system to short-cut the supercharger at the top end. It was an amazing but complex system which worked remarkably well in practice.

The Delta S4 was designed in 1983, unveiled in December 1984, homologated on 1 November in 1985 and won its first event – the British RAC International rally – just a few days later. In 1986 it won the Monte Carlo rally and other top-flight events, but its burgeoning career was cut short by the cancellation of rallying's Group B category.

Lancia built 200 well equipped and remarkably civilized Delta S4 road cars in 1985, which were not intended to be used in motor sport. These have now all become collectors' items and, like the Ford RS200 and Peugeot 205 Turbo 16 models, are exhilarating if rather noisy cars for road use.

RIGHT Lancia designed the Delta S4 to be a Rally-winning Group B 'special', needing only to produce 200 cars to qualify for the category. The S4 won its first-ever World Championship event, the British Lombard-RAC of 1985, and followed it up by winning in 1986 at Monte Carlo. As a brand-new four-wheel-drive supercar, with turbocharging *and* supercharging, it was a great success.

BELOW RIGHT As the dust clouds prove, all four wheels of the Delta S4 were driven. The turbo/supercharged engine was behind the seats, and although the car looked superficially like that of the Delta production car, there was no mechanical comparison.

BELOW, FAR RIGHT The Delta S4 was a special car, designed for a special purpose. Several types of front spoiler, rear aerodynamic aids, front/rear drive splits, and turbos matched to superchargers, were all tried before the Martini-sponsored team was satisfied.

LANCIA
DELTA HF 4WD

PRODUCTION SPAN
Introduced 1986

ENGINE
4 cyl, Twin ohc

CAPACITY
122 CID/1,995cc

MAXIMUM POWER
165bhp

CHASSIS/SUSPENSION
Steel unit-construction
body/chassis structure,
coil spring and
MacPherson strut ifs,
coil spring and
MacPherson strut irs

BODY STYLE
4 door 5 seater saloon

TOP SPEED
128mph/205kph

0-60MPH
6.6 seconds

In 1985 and 1986 the Lancia 'works' rally team used Delta S4 cars in the Group B category, whereas from the beginning of 1987 it used the Group A Delta HF 4WD models instead. Because the colour schemes did not change (Martini were the main sponsors) you could be excused for thinking that the cars were closely related – in fact the only similarity was in the body style.

Fiat had taken over Lancia in 1969. In the late 1970s Fiat had launched the new Ritmo-Strada front-drive hatchback car, and it was on the basis of this car's running gear that Lancia then produced the new and crisply styled Delta hatchback in 1979. As with the Ritmo there was a choice of transversely mounted engines, the most powerful of which were the medium sized twin-cam types as pioneered in the 1960s for the Fiat 124s, and later redeveloped for front-wheel-drive installation.

By the early 1980s Lancia had also evolved the Prisma model, a 'booted' version of the Delta, which was the car first given a new and simple four-wheel-drive 'conversion', linked to a 108bhp 97 CID/1.6 litre normally aspirated version of the famous twin-cam engine. This was so versatile that it had been carburetted, fuel-injected, subjected to a turbo conversion in the USA and also built in Volumex supercharged form for other Fiats and Lancias.

In June 1986 the 'hot-rod' derivative of the same basic chassis, the Delta HF 4WD, was introduced. Not only did this car use the same four-wheel-drive system, complete with a centre viscous coupling differential, and a rear Torsen differential, but the engine was a turbocharged version of the larger size 122 CID/1,995cc twin-cam, producing no less than 165bhp.

One benefit of rationalization was that this engine was really a slightly modified version of that already fitted to the larger Thema model, complete with twin counter-rotating balance shafts to make it even smoother. The turbocharger was a Garrett T3, allowed to develop a peak boost of 12.8psi/0.9 Bar. The turbo itself was ideally positioned in the engine bay, between the front grille and the cylinder block. There was an air-air intercooler close by, right behind the grille, and although the engine bay was well filled, it was a very effective package which soon proved to be capable of developing 240bhp (later 260bhp) in 'Group A' rally tune. The 16 valve head used on earlier competition engines was not, however, used on this car.

Compared with some of its rivals, both in the market place and on rally circuits of the world, the Delta HF 4WD was a light, compact and nicely developed design. In spite of protests to the contrary by factory spokesmen, it seems certain that Lancia had always intended to use it as a competition car, and it proved its worth right away.

It won its first major event – Monte Carlo 1987 – and was completely dominant in World Championship rallying in 1987, winning both the Manufacturers series, and providing motive power for the winner of the Drivers series, Juha Kankkunen.

Although the Delta HF 4WD looked similar to the Delta S4, the two cars had nothing in common. The HF 4WD had a front-mounted turbocharged engine, and a simple four-wheel-drive system, and was built around a pressed-steel monocoque with four passenger doors. Even so, Lancia soon turned it into a successful rally car, winning the World Rally Championship of 1987.

LEFT Two very different Deltas compared – the blue car is a standard production HF 4WD, and the one in Martini colours is the 'works' rally car. Road cars developed 165bhp, but the Group A Rally cars produced 250bhp. Both used the same type of turbocharged 4-cylinder 2-litre engine.

ABOVE LEFT The Delta HF 4WD had a neat style by Giugiaro, and featured a transversely-mounted front engine, plus four-wheel-drive. Other, less expensive Deltas, had smaller engines, and front-wheel-drive.

ABOVE AND RIGHT Although the badging of the Delta HF4WD is clear enough, there is no mention of a turbocharged engine. On the open road, however, the performance makes that very clear indeed . . .

LOTUS ESPRIT TURBO

PRODUCTION SPAN
Introduced 1980

–

ENGINE
4 cyl, Twin ohc

–

CAPACITY
133 CID/2,174cc

–

MAXIMUM POWER
210bhp

–

CHASSIS/SUSPENSION
Steel backbone-style
chassis frame, with
GRP body shell, coil
spring and wishbone
ifs, coil spring and
wishbone irs

–

BODY STYLE
2 door 2 seater coupé

–

TOP SPEED
148mph/229kph

–

0-60MPH
6.1 seconds

–

Starting in 1974 with the new Elite hatchback, Lotus began the complete renewal of its product range. The third model in this range, launched in 1975 but not going on sale until the summer of 1976, was the mid-engined Esprit. As with all previous Lotus road cars these were designed with function rather than accommodation as the first priority, and all had body shells made from glass fibre.

All these cars were powered by the same powerful and brand new engine. This was an alloy four cylinder unit, complete with twin overhead camshafts, 16 valves and two twin-choke carburettors. At first this was a 120 CID 2.0 litre design, but from 1980 (as a response to the demand for more power and torque and also to help tailor the engine to future exhaust emission controls) the engine was enlarged to 133 CID/2,174cc. Because it was really only half of a projected V8 engine design, it was installed in the new cars at an angle of 45 degrees.

The mid-engined Esprit had a steel backbone chassis, a Citroen SM-type five-speed gearbox, and a distinctive coupé body style in GRP by Giugiaro of Italy. Perhaps this body's drag coefficient was not as low as Lotus would have hoped, for road test cars with 160bhp were not capable of the 135mph claimed by the factory, nor was the original 120 CID/2.0 litre engine a very torquey unit. The long stroke 133 CID/2.2 litre engine, therefore, was the first response to this.

Although the Esprit had a small passenger cabin, and very restricted luggage space, it was also a car which looked sensational and handled like a de-tuned racing car which, in effect, it was. It was a small though not very light car (13ft/9in/419cm long, but weighing 2,653lb/1,203kg), it could be steered to fractions of an inch and it was as nimble as any single seater race car.

However, it was to turn the Esprit from a fast coupé into a startlingly fast supercar that Lotus then developed a turbocharged version introduced in 1980. Surprisingly the twin-choke carburettor installation (Dellorto DHLA in this case) was retained. A Garrett T3 turbocharger was mounted behind the cylinder block, where there was plenty of space in the engine bay, and Lotus never thought it necessary to develop or install an intercooler.

The result was a 210bhp engine which pushed the newly named Esprit Turbo up to a near 150mph maximum speed, and gave the car Porsche Turbo-like performance at a fraction of the cost. Not only that but the car seemed to suffer only slightly from turbo lag; it was this excellent development achievement that helped launch Lotus into the consultant engineering field.

The Esprit's body style was completely revised in the autumn of 1987, with a more rounded shape introduced, but the much-rumoured and intriguing V8 version of the engine had still not progressed beyond the prototype stage.

RIGHT Giugiaro collaborated with Lotus to produce this stunning Esprit style in the mid-1970s, but it did not appear in turbocharged form until 1980. The Esprit had a steel backbone frame, a glass fibre body shell and a mid-mounted engine.

BELOW RIGHT The turbocharged 2-litre engine of the Esprit produced up to 210bhp, without the help of an intercooler. Extra cooling air was fed in through ducts in the sills and there were slots, rather than a pane of glass, over the mid-mounted engine.

OVERLEAF, TOP LEFT The Giugiaro style for the Esprit was at once low, sleek, and functional. The screen sloped back at a near impossible angle, and the engine was tucked into the space behind the seats but ahead of the rear wheels.

OVERLEAF, BOTTOM LEFT In the early 1980s, Lotus not only gained world-wide publicity from its Grand Prix race cars, but from its connections with the *James Bond* films. This study links an '007' Esprit Turbo with chairman Colin Chapman's appropriately-registered 'plane.

OVERLEAF, TOP RIGHT For night-driving the Esprit's headlamps could be popped up. The car's nose was fashionably low and wedge-shaped.

OVERLEAF, BOTTOM RIGHT It is impossible to confuse the Esprit with another car from any angle. Experts could pick out a Turbo by its unique styling details, its ultra-wide tyres, and by its sheer performance. The handling, as you might expect of a Lotus sports car, was precise and responsive.

MASERATI BITURBO

PRODUCTION SPAN
Introduced 1981

ENGINE
V6 cyl, ohc

CAPACITY
122/152/170 CID/1,996/
2,491/2,790cc

MAXIMUM POWER
180/200/220/250bhp

CHASSIS/SUSPENSION
Steel unit-construction
body/chassis structure,
coil spring and
MacPherson strut ifs,
coil spring and semi-
trailing arm irs

BODY STYLE
2 door or 4 door
4 seater coupe, saloon
or 'Spider'

TOP SPEED
(2.5 litre/200bhp
version)
126mph/202kph

0-60MPH
(2.5 litre/200bhp
version) 7.2 seconds

The 1980s generation of Maseratis was conceived and masterminded by Alejandro DeTomaso, who had bought up the bankrupt Italian supercar concern in 1975. Except in the use of its name, and the famous trident grille badge, this Maserati was completely different from any previous model.

In the late 1970s DeTomaso came to the pragmatic view that Maserati was never likely to rebuild its image sufficiently to beat Ferrari and Lamborghini in a straight fight. Accordingly he decided to see a new generation of 'mini-supercar' Maseratis developed – smaller engined and much cheaper, if not technically more simple, than the old-style Maseratis. With planned (and as it transpired achieved) production volumes of more than 5,000 cars a year, DeTomaso intended to sell more cars than Ferrari, and to reach an entirely different sector of the motoring market.

Structurally and visually the new Maserati was conventional enough, for it had a front engine and rear drive, a pressed steel unit-construction monocoque and positively under-stated styling by Maserati itself. Right from the start a whole range of designs – closed and open, two door and four door, were planned for this design, though different wheelbases (the Spider being shortest the four door saloon the longest) were used on every model. By late 1980s standards the front of the cars was bluff and not at all aerodynamic: this is confirmed by the performance figures, which show flashing low speed acceleration but disappointing top speeds.

The new car's name – Biturbo – gave a very strong clue to the new type of engine chosen for these cars. Not only was it a V6 unit, with turbocharging, but the cylinder vee-angle was 90 degrees, rather than the 60 degrees which is more usual, and there were two turbochargers and three valves per cylinder. All main engine castings were in light alloy, there was a single overhead camshaft for each bank of cylinders, with two inlet valves, one small one larger than the other.

DeTomaso was as ever, technically adventurous, for the engine featured one small turbocharger (a water cooled Japanese IHI) per cylinder bank, mounted low down under the exhaust manifold and feeding pressurized air up to the 'carburation'. This was by Weber carburettors in the case of the 'basic' 180bhp 122/CID 2 litre engine, but fuel injection, and sometimes catalyzers, were used in other cases, depending on engine size and the market for which the car was to be sold.

The 180bhp 2 litre had no intercooler, but the more powerful 220bhp 'S' had an air-air intercooler to cool the pressurized air.

In the first five years of its existence the Biturbo range expanded considerably and became more diverse. Originally only a 2 door coupé with 122 CID/2.0 litre engine was offered, but this was joined by a 152 CID/2·5 litre engine option, and a four door saloon, available from the end of 1983. The Spider (with a body shell by Zagato) arrived at the end of 1984 and fuel injected engines followed in 1986. The 228 coupé, with 170 CID/2.8 litre engine, was launched at the end of 1984.

DeTomaso's strategy certainly succeeded, for by the late 1980s Maserati was making more cars than ever before in its history.

RIGHT The BiTurbo was launched in 1981, not only the smallest Maserati for many years, but the very first to have a turbocharged engine. Maserati's new owner, Alejandro DeTomaso, wanted to take Maserati downmarket, and to increase sales: the BiTurbo was an ideal new model to do this for him.

INSET The BiTurbo's interior was compact, but sumptuously furnished, with room for four passengers.

BELOW RIGHT While not as low, nor as flamboyantly styled, as 1960s and 1970s-style Maseratis, the twin-turbocharged BiTurbo was smart and attractive. Sales of Maseratis soared in the mid-1980s.

MAZDA 323 TURBO 4WD

PRODUCTION SPAN
Introduced 1985

ENGINE
4 cyl, Twin ohc

CAPACITY
97.5 CID/1,597cc

MAXIMUM POWER
148bhp

CHASSIS/SUSPENSION
Steel unit-construction
body/chassis structure,
coil spring and
MacPherson strut ifs,
coil spring and
MacPherson strut ifs

BODY STYLE
3 door 4 seater
hatchback

TOP SPEED
120mph/192kph

0–60MPH
7.9 seconds

During the 1970s Mazda forged technical and financial links with Ford, the result being that the new (second generation) Mazda 323 of 1980 had many features (if not actual components) in common with the original front-wheel-drive Ford Escort. By 1985 however Mazda was ready to go its own way before Ford was ready for a change, so the third generation 323 was a unique design, with engines ranging from 74bhp/79 CID/1.3 litre unit to 105bhp/97.5 CID/1.6 litres, along with a diesel powered alternative.

In the autumn of 1985 however Mazda surprised and intrigued the motoring world with an exciting derivative of the latest 323 model. Not only did it have four-wheel-drive but power came from a new turbocharged twin-cam four cylinder engine. Nor was this a limited production model, for sporting homologation was achieved within months (which meant that 5,000 examples had been produced) and before long the cars were being entered in World Championship rallies. The first big win came in the Swedish rally of February 1987.

The car's styling was typically modern Japanese – compact, rounded and with a long line-up of features as standard equipment. For the super-sporting application there were two tailgate spoilers – one immediately aft of the top hinges, the other around the base of the rear window. Alloy wheels and a deeper front spoiler helped to complete an appealing package. The engine, like all others fitted to this range of cars, was transversely mounted, the main gearbox being mounted alongside it and towards the left side of the car.

Linked to the five speed transmission, through its final drive, was a simple take off to a propeller shaft leading to the rear axle. The torque split was 50/50, and the centre diff. was lockable by operating a dashboard switch; so much power could be developed by rally-tuned engines that this transmission tended to give trouble and stronger versions were developed during 1987. Suspension was by MacPherson struts all round, with disc brakes at front and rear, and power-assisted steering was standard.

The fascinating new engine was a rugged design, with a cast iron cylinder block, an alloy head and twin overhead-camshafts driven by a cogged belt and four valves per cylinder operated via hydraulic tappets; fuel injection was by licence-built Bosch L-Jetronic. The turbocharger was a Japanese IHI RHB 5 type down at the front of the engine, behind the water radiator, and there was an air-air intercooler alongside that water radiator, immediately behind the front grille. Peak boost was a modest 8.1 psi/0.57 Bar.

This turbocharged four-wheel-drive Mazda was just one of several indications that the Japanese motor industry could match, and surpass, the Europeans and the Americans in all aspects of car design. By most other Mazda standards (if not the RX-7) it was a fast and very nimble car which sold well in Japan, Europe and the United States. Other such Mazdas must surely follow in the years to come.

RIGHT Japanese style and engineering has come a long way since the copy-cat days of the 1960s. Mazda's 323 was essentially a mass-market front-wheel-drive car, but the Turbo 4WD also had four-wheel-drive and a powerful twin-cam turbocharged engine. The Turbo 4WD car was competitive in Group A rallying in 1987, though plagued by a weak transmission.

LEFT There was really no space for *anything* else under the bonnet of the 323 Turbo 4WD. The twin-cam engine sits transversely, the turbocharger is at the front of the engine bay, and the air-air intercooler is alongside it.

MAZDA RX-7 2.6 LITRE TURBO

PRODUCTION SPAN
Introduced in 1985
–
ENGINE
2-rotor Wankel rotary
–
CAPACITY
160 CID/2,616cc
(nominal)
–
MAXIMUM POWER
185bhp
–
CHASSIS/SUSPENSION
Steel unit-construction
body/chassis structure,
coil spring and
MacPherson strut ifs,
coil spring and semi-
trailing arm irs
–
BODY STYLE
2 door 2 seater
hatchback coupé
–
TOP SPEED
143mph/229kph
–
0–60MPH
7.0 seconds
–

Felix Wankel's rotary engine promised much in the early 1960s when it was taken up by so many companies. NSU of West Germany and Mazda of Japan pioneered the use of such engines in production cars but by the early 1970s the engine's reputation was in ruins. Poor reliability and poor fuel consumption caused all but Mazda to abandon development; the Japanese company has continued to build Wankel-engined cars to the present day.

Mazda's sleek new Wankel-engined sports coupé, the RX-7, was launched in 1978 and immediately made its mark, particularly in the USA where it was seen as modern, beautiful and above all fashionable. Not only was the RX-7 a smart car offering the same sort of performance, image and accommodation as the Porsche 924, but it used a well developed version of Mazda's twin-rotor Wankel engine.

The second-generation RX-7, which was also called 'Savanna' in certain countries, was launched in 1985. Not only was it cleaner, smoother and more aerodynamic in style than the original, but it was targeted even more squarely at the potential Porsche 924 customers. The first generation RX-7s used engines with a nominal capacity of 140 CID/2,292cc, but the new generation model used an enlarged engine of 160 CID/2,616cc. A turbocharged 140 CID/2.3 litre Wankel engine was made available from the end of 1983.

Most new-model RX-7s had normally aspirated engines, fuelled by Bosch L-Jetronic fuel injection. In this form they had 150bhp, and could urge the 2,700lb/1,225kg coupé up to 134mph. However the 'flagship' of the new RX-7/Savanna range was a turbocharged version, which boosted peak power to 185bhp, and top speeds to nearly 145mph/230kph. The turbo was a scrolled type, jointly developed with Hitachi, and the latest version of the rotary engine had additional inlet ports to improve the breathing.

The turbo engine not only gave the RX-7 a great deal more power and torque than its normally aspirated relative, but it also made the car completely competitive with the latest small Porsches – the 924S and 944 models. The RX-7's lengthy engine bay made the inclusion of the turbocharger, and an air-air intercooler, a straightforward business.

By any standards – Japanese, North American or European – the second-generation RX-7 was an appealing package. Although the fixed-head coupé style was provided with a very cramped pair of 'occasional' seats it was better to treat it as a two seater, there being no legroom at all in the rear if the front seats were pushed back.

The chassis had MacPherson strut suspension at the front, and semi-trailing arms at the rear; Mazda's DTSS (Dynamic Tracking Suspension System) was claimed to adjust rear suspension toe-in and toe-out very slightly during cornering maneouvres, yet testers sometimes suggested that it made the car actually feel less secure than a conventional system would do.

In general however the RX-7's good looks, spirited performance and high-quality construction made it very popular; a new convertible version was launched in 1987 to make the car even more attractive for Californian customers.

RIGHT One look at the lines of the RX-7 Turbo, and a drag coefficient of 0.31 comes as no surprise; there was plenty of room under the bonnet for the turbo and, located over the engine, the air-air intercooler.

MIDDLE, FAR RIGHT ABS (anti-lock brake system) was an option for the RX-7 Turbo. Electromagnetic sensors at each wheel relayed braking action to a microprocessor which modulated braking to avoid wheel lock-up and improve stability. With a quarter-mile time of just 15.2 seconds, it was probably a good option to take.

MIDDLE RIGHT The turbo was designed to combat turbo lag by working in two stages; at low revs, a primary chamber was open, with the gases concentrated on sections of the turbine blades. Above 2,500 rpm, the second chamber opened, driving all of the blades' surfaces.

BOTTOM On the hatchback version, the sunroof was standard; and a neat package it was too, sliding back without encroaching on the headroom inside.

MERCEDES-BENZ
300TD TURBO

PRODUCTION SPAN
Introduced in 1984

ENGINE
6 cyl, ohc

CAPACITY
183 CID/2,998cc Diesel

MAXIMUM POWER
143bhp

CHASSIS/SUSPENSION
Steel unit-construction
body/chassis structure,
coil spring and
MacPherson strut ifs,
coil spring and multi-
link irs

BODY STYLE
4 door 5 seater
saloon or estate

TOP SPEED
120mph/192kph

0-60MPH
Not recorded

Not only is Mercedes-Benz a very prolific manufacturer of automotive diesel engines today, but it was also the very first manufacturer to put a diesel-engined car on sale – in 1936. After the Second World War more and more four cylinder diesel-engined Mercedes-Benz cars were built; because of this the marque even acquired the slightly condescending nickname of the 'Stuttgart taxi'.

However the Swabian manufacturer's great leap forward came in 1974 when it introduced the world's first passenger-car five cylinder engine. This was diesel-powered, and a few years later, to keep it competitive in USA markets, the same engine was turbocharged as well.

The company announced a new range of medium sized (by Mercedes-Benz standards – but large by any other reckoning) cars in 1984, these being the W124 models. As you might expect from this super-thorough West German manufacturer a complete range of cars, engines and sub-derivatives was available right from the start.

Not only were there four and six cylinder petrol powered engines, ranging from 105bhp to 180bhp, but there was a complete range of diesels. This was a complex offering for there were four, five and six-cylinder diesels, all being derived from the same general design. Not only that, but at the top of the range there was a turbocharged version of the 'six', a very powerful 143bhp 183 CID/2,998cc unit.

The car carrying this engine was dubbed 300TD Turbo and was, without a doubt, the world's fastest diesel-engined car when launched. Mercedes-Benz claimed a top speed of at least 120mph, though in the USA where this engine/car combination was most popular the cars were obliged to trundle along at a mere 55mph, which was the USA's infamous 'Double Nickel' speed limit at the time.

The W124 range was solidly built and carefully developed, yet it had a very low-drag body style (Cd = 0.30), and advanced all-independent suspension. The diesel engines all had light-alloy cylinder heads and were machined on the same transfer lines. The 300TD's turbocharger was by Garrett and was matched to multi-point Bosch fuel injection. The compression ratio was high, at 22.0:1. There was no intercooler.

Although the big diesel engine was heavy the 300TD felt very well balanced, and it was certainly a lot faster than one might expect of such a machine. Even though the saloon car itself was quite heavy, at 3,375lb/1,530kg, it felt not only safe and secure but it also had very spritely handling. It certainly was a car to improve the image of diesel engined cars – it was no wonder that Mercedes-Benz completely dominated the diesel market in the USA in the 1980s.

The same engine was also offered from autumn 1985 in the largest Mercedes-Benz saloon, sold exclusively in the United States and badged 300SDL Turbodiesel.

Modern turbo-diesel engined Mercedes-Benz cars come in all sizes, with a definite family likeness. Five cylinder *and* six-cylinder diesels were built on the same 'modular' basis. The sectioned engine (bottom) was the turbocharged six, of 2,998cc, which was canted over so that it could fit neatly in a crowded engine bay. The '300D' model title (inset, top right) denotes a 3-litre engine, diesel-powered.

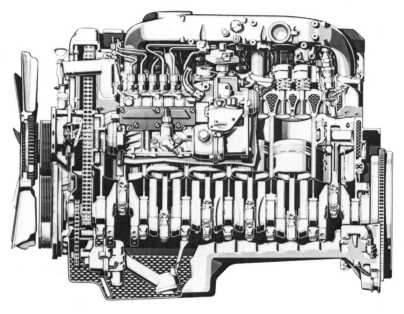

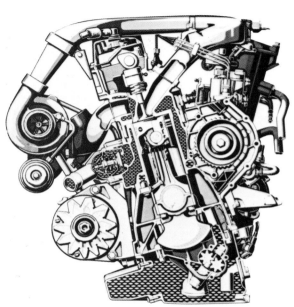

MERKUR XR4Ti

PRODUCTION SPAN
Introduced in 1984

—

ENGINE
4 cyl, ohc

—

CAPACITY
140 CID/2,301cc

—

MAXIMUM POWER
145/175bhp

—

CHASSIS/SUSPENSION
Steel unit-construction
body/chassis structure,
coil spring and
MacPherson strut ifs,
coil spring and semi-
trailing arm irs

—

BODY STYLE
2 door 5 seater saloon

—

TOP SPEED
(175bhp version)
127mph/203kph

—

0-60MPH
8.0 seconds

—

Merkur is a modern marque invented by Ford-USA, to identify a car designed and built in Europe but sold in North America. The XR4Ti was an interesting mixture of European chassis and structural engineering allied to an American turbocharged engine, all assembled by a specialist coachbuilder.

The main roots of the Merkur come from the European Ford Sierra motor car, and from the American four-cylinder 'Lima' turbocharged engine used in a whole variety of Ford-USA products in the mid and late 1980s. The practical reason for the marriage was that Ford wanted to sell the most sporty types of Sierra in the USA but did not have a suitable European engine. The 'Lima' engine was already 'de-toxed' for use in emissions conscious North America and could easily be slotted into place.

Ford's new 1980s-style medium-sized car was the Sierra range, a family of front engine/rear drive models with controversial rounded (but wind-cheating) styling. The fastest of these cars, put on sale in 1983, was the XR4i model which was powered by the long-established 170 CID/2.8 litre V6 engine and equipped with a distinctive 'bi-plane' type of rear spoiler; the body shell had only two passenger doors.

For sale in the USA, and the most emissions-conscious European countries only, Ford matched this distinctive car to the 'Lima' engine and the five-speed Borg Warner transmission which had already been put on sale in the Mustang SVO. Without a doubt this car was meant to be a fast sports saloon and its styling ensured that it was always marketed in this way.

Compared with the XR4i from which it was developed the XR4Ti (T = Turbocharger no doubt) handled better in all respects, and where speed limits allowed could be driven very quickly indeed. In race-tuned form the XR4Ti was very successful in British, European and North American touring car races.

In manual transmission form, with an intercooler, the engine developed 175bhp and for a time there was also a 145bhp version (another existing Mustang engine tune) for use with automatic transmission. As with the Mustang applications the 'Lima' engine featured single-overhead-cam valve gear operation, hydraulic tappets and electronic fuel injection. The most powerful version developed no less than 14 psi/1.0 Bar of boost from its Garrett turbocharger.

Construction of the bodies, and final assembly of the cars, was carried out for Ford by Karmann of West Germany, the engines and transmissions being shipped over from the USA in bulk for installation in the cars, and for re-export to the USA! Sales in the USA were handled by Ford's Lincoln-Mercury Division, the name of 'Merkur' being sufficiently close to 'Mercury' for the two cars to be linked together.

Sales began at the end of 1984 and soon built up to a range of 15,000 cars a year, even though Ford had some problems in establishing a discrete identity with its clientele. The suspension and wheel designs were updated for 1987, and a new single-spoiler tailgate was adopted for 1988.

The Merkur was sold almost exclusively in the USA, has an American turbocharged engine, but was assembled in Europe. The body and suspension was a modified version of the Ford Sierra XR4i style of the early 1980s, with two passenger doors. Early examples had bi-plane rear spoilers, but for 1988 these were replaced by a simple single spoiler. By any standards the Merkur was a fast and agile sports saloon.

MG METRO TURBO

PRODUCTION SPAN
Introduced in 1982

ENGINE
4 cyl, ohv

CAPACITY
78 CID/1,275cc

MAXIMUM POWER
93bhp

CHASSIS/SUSPENSION
Steel unit-construction body/chassis structure, Hydragas spring/wishbone ifs, Hydragas spring and trailing arm irs

BODY STYLE
2 door 4 seater saloon

TOP SPEED
110mph/176kph

0-60MPH
9.4 seconds

Like many marketing decisions made by Austin-Rover in the early 1980s, the thinking behind the launch of the MG Metro Turbo was somewhat obscure. The car was not a 'homologation special', built with motor sport in mind, and it was neither fast enough nor trendy enough to be a 'GTI-beater'. But it was a very competently engineered, and very brisk, sporty little hatchback.

During the 1970s, Austin-Rover's ancestors (British Leyland – later BL Cars) had struggled to evolve a new small car, to take over effectively from the ancient Mini. Project after project was started then abandoned, and it was not until 1980 that a new car, called the Austin Metro, was actually launched.

The Metro, while larger and heavier than the Mini (which was and is still manufactured), was a more practical car in many ways, not least in that it had much more space inside, and it was a hatchback model. Like the Mini the new Metro retained the same transverse engine and front-wheel-drive transmission. In 1959, when originally launched, this had been hailed as a miracle of packaging; its one significant disadvantage was that the gearbox was positioned under, rather than alongside, the engine and there was only space for four forward gears to be installed.

Original Metros had a choice of 61 CID/998cc and 78 CID/1,275cc engines, the most powerful version producing 63bhp. Then, in the spring of 1982, a more up-market 1300 with much higher quality seats, trim and equipment, called an MG Metro, was introduced, with 73bhp and a top speed of 100mph.

Six months later the turbocharged version of this car was announced. Visually it was nearly identical to the normally aspirated MG Metro 1300, and its engine was a carefully reworked version of the old 'A-Series' 1,275cc engine (an engine size first seen in BMC cars in 1964).

Much of the turbocharging development work had been carried out under contract by Lotus. There were two important restraints – one was the physical one, in that there was very little space in the engine bay, and both the inlet and exhaust systems were tucked away behind the engine where they could not really benefit from cold air being pushed in through the front grille; the other was that they were obliged to retain a single SU carburettor and the standard cylinder head, which had siamesed inlet ports. There was no intercooler – the layout of the engine bay would have made this an impractical fitting.

The Garrett T3 turbocharger was matched to a surprisingly high compression ratio of 9.4:1 (the same as the normally aspirated MG Metro), and was limited to supply 7.7 psi/0.54 Bar of boost. This was arranged, not only by conventional means, but by more complex electronic limiters taking note of a variety of signals, including that of engine speed, and low speed boost was limited to 4 psi/0.28 Bar below 4,500rpm.

Because the MG Metro's gearbox had certain torque limitations which could not be improved (the lack of space was, once again, the reason), the boost was arranged to improve markedly above 4,500rpm, when the torque was already falling away – for maximum torque was actually developed at 2,650rpm – which is very low for this type of engine.

Except that Austin-Rover promoted one-make racing championships for these cars, the Metro Turbo was not used in competition and sold steadily, if not spectacularly, as a fast and unobtrusive road car.

RIGHT This was Austin-Rover's very first turbocharged production car, introduced in 1982. It had a transversely-mounted engine, driving the front wheels; the turbocharging conversion of the old A Plus engine was carried out by Lotus.

INSET The Metro Turbo's styling was almost the same as that of other Metros, except that it had turbo badging, and decals on the flanks.

ABOVE The tailgate spoiler on Metros was functional, not cosmetic, for it helped restrict the drag and also kept dirt off the rear window.

RIGHT MG and 'Turbo' – one of the motor industry's most famous names, linked to one of the most exciting engine developments of the modern era.

TOP LEFT Modern MG styling motifs included red piping around both the doors and seats . . .

MIDDLE LEFT . . . along with red badging on the steering wheel. There was no turbo boost gauge on the instrument panel, and the rev-counter's 'red-line' started at 6,000rpm.

LEFT The engine package was one of the few modern units to combine turbocharging with a carburettor (rather than fuel injection). The turbo was hidden under the carburettor, behind the engine block, and away from the cooling air streaming in through the grille.

ABOVE For such a small car, the MG Metro Turbo was equipped with sumptuously trimmed sports seats.

MITSUBISHI COLT STARION

PRODUCTION SPAN
Introduced in 1982

ENGINE
4 cyl, ohc

CAPACITY
122 CID/1,997cc

MAXIMUM POWER
168/177bhp

CHASSIS/SUSPENSION
Steel unit-construction
body/chassis structure,
coil spring and
MacPherson strut ifs,
coil spring and
MacPhersons strut irs

BODY STYLE
2 door 2+2 seater coupé

TOP SPEED
133mph/213kph

0-60MPH
7.5/6.9 seconds

The very first Mitsubishi car was produced in 1917, just one of many products being developed by Japan's mighty industrial colossus. However there was a lengthy withdrawal from car-making after the Second World War and the company did not re-enter the business until 1959. After that car manufacture expanded rapidly, and links were forged with the Chrysler Corporation in the early 1970s.

Mitsubishi (like Nissan) came to export more and more cars to the USA, where it rapidly became jealous of Porche's sales success and sporting image. Although the company had produced several turbo-charged passenger cars by the early 1980s, it had never built a special-ized sports coupé. Then, in 1982, it surprised the world of motoring by launching the new Starion coupé.

The Starion name was derived from 'Star Orion' and is supposed to be derived from 'stellar', though the car itself was rather more down to earth. The basis of the 'chassis' was the existing Galant/Sapporo model range, the five-speed gearbox was that of the Galant/Sapporo, while the 122 CID/2.0 litre four cylinder engine was that already found in the Turbo Lancer. The style was conventional early 1980s – with a wedge nose, flip-up headlamps, a hatchback, and rather cramped four seater coupé accommodation best described as '2+2'. In its original form it was quite a narrow car, but by the late 1970s the style had been revised to have Audi Quattro-like wheel arch flares, linked to larger diameter and wider rim wheels.

The Starion's most outstanding feature, without a doubt, was its four-cylinder engine. Although superficially this looked like any other in-line 'four', it had many intriguing features. Not only did it have single over-head-camshaft valve gear, driven by an internally cogged belt, but there were additional counter-rotating balancer shafts to make it significantly smoother than conventional four cylinder engines.

The turbocharger was Mitsubishi's own unit, which directed the boosted charge across the top of the engine to what Mitsubishi called an ECI (Electronic Control Injection unit) – this looked like a sealed carburettor but was actually a complex sensoring and metering unit which governed fuel flow into fuel injectors. Maximum turbo boost was 8.5 psi/0.6 Bar. This was a typically different Japanese solution to a complex series of turbocharging problems, and on the road it certainly seemed to work well. There was no intercooler on the first cars, but this was added in 1985, which helped to boost the power output.

The Starion was a very lively car, and was successful in certain categories of production car racing. Testers described it as a real 'fun' car, not only because of the terrific punch provided by the turbocharged engine, but because the chassis had excellent roadholding and fabulous brakes.

The revised Starion was intended to give an even better chassis platform than before and succeeded in this intent, though there was still quite a bit of turbo lag because very little torque was developed below 3,500rpm. Even so it was much the most exciting car so far designed by Mitsubishi.

RIGHT The Starion was not only a fast 2+2 seater sports coupe, but it also became a very effective racing car. The standard road car engine produced 168bhp, but up to 300bhp was possible in racing tune.

BELOW RIGHT The Starion's engine was a 2-litre overhead-cam design, used in atmospheric *and* turbocharged form in different Mitsubishi models.

BELOW, FAR RIGHT Should the Starion have been called a Stallion, and did the Japanese get it wrong in 1982 when the new car was launched? Maybe – but the car was just as fast, no matter what it was called.

NISSAN FAIRLADY Z/300ZX

PRODUCTION SPAN
Introduced in 1983

ENGINE
V6 cyl, ohc

CAPACITY
189 CID/2,960cc

MAXIMUM POWER
195/255bhp

CHASSIS/SUSPENSION
Steel unit-construction
body/chassis structure,
coil spring and
MacPherson strut ifs,
coil spring and semi-
trailing arm irs

BODY STYLE
2 door 2 seater or
2+2 seater coupé

TOP SPEED
(225bhp model)
143mph/229kph

0-60MPH
(225bhp model)
7.0 seconds

This is a complex tale of options and nomenclature. Many years ago Nissan built cars badged as Datsuns, and it is only in the 1980s that this name has been dropped. This means that the company's famous series of Z-Cars, which began with the 240Z in 1969, started life as Datsuns and are now universally known as Nissans.

From 1969 to 1983 Nissan built two distinctly different series of Z-Cars, all with in-line six cylinder engines, and with a choice of two seater or 2+2 seater bodywork. Every Z-Car had all-round independent suspension, and from 1978 there were four-wheel disc brakes. Later models had the option of a 'Targa' type of coupé body, with lift-off glass panels above the occupants' heads. The cars soon became big sellers in the United States and it was with that vast and prosperous market in mind that the third generation Z-Car, known by Nissan as the Z31 series, was launched in 1983.

Even after so much time there was still confusion over names, for the new car had different names in different markets. All however shared the same impressive style, and were faster and technically more advanced than their predecessors. As before, there were two seater and 2+2 seater types.

Although the new car was a direct replacement for the 280ZX of 1978–1983 it was different in almost every way. In particular Nissan were faced with strong competition from Toyota, and had needed a new engine for some time. The heart of the latest car therefore was Nissan's latest VG type of engine, a 60-degree V6 unit of 181 CID/2,960cc with single overhead camshaft valve gear, operated via rockers and hydraulic tappets.

It was an engine intended for use in other sizes, and in other Nissan models, but for the 300ZX it was given Bosch-type electronic fuel injection and turbocharging. The turbo was of Garrett TO3 type, though Nissan manufactured its own housings and controls, and peak boost was 7 psi/0.48 Bar. It was mounted low down on the left side of the engine. Perhaps it was as well that Nissan did not specify a charge intercooler as the front of the car was already well filled with water cooling and air conditioning radiators.

The engine was offered for sale in a relatively 'soft' state of tune, with 195 bhp (DIN) for most markets, but with 225bhp for European countries where exhaust emission controls were not as strictly applied.

Other engine types were also made available for the car, none with as much power and torque – a 122 CID/2 litre V6 Turbo unit for Japan only, a different 122 CID/2 litre in-line six with turbocharging and twin overhead-camshafts, and from 1986 a 181 CID/3 litre V6 with four valves per cylinder, twin overhead-camshafts, but normal aspiration, and with 190bhp . . .

All these sporting Nissans were bulky, comfortable, heavy and unmistakably Oriental in their style, yet they were clearly aimed at export markets. At first their handling was too soft, their looks were too bland and their manners too 'boulevard' to be truly enjoyable, but from 1986 Nissan gave the car a facelift by softening the lines, tautening-up the chassis and making it feel more sporting once again. Annual sales exceeded 70,000 cars which made the 300ZX a 'best-seller' by any sports car standard.

RIGHT Nissan's Fairlady for the 1980s was the third generation of this type, and used a massively powerful turbocharged V6 engine. Styling was strictly home-grown, and the car was sold in 2+2 or two-seater guise.

RIGHT A thoughtful and elegant styling touch was the shaping of the wheels to resemble turbines.

OLDSMOBILE F85 JETFIRE

PRODUCTION SPAN
1962 and 1963

ENGINE
V8 cyl, ohv

CAPACITY
215 CID/3,528cc

MAXIMUM POWER
215bhp

CHASSIS/SUSPENSION
Steel unit-construction
body/chassis structure,
coil spring and wishbone
ifs, coil spring and
radius arm rear beam

BODY STYLE
2 door 5 seater coupé

TOP SPEED
107mph/171kph

0-60MPH
8.5 seconds

It is not generally realised that General Motors of North America was the first to put turbocharged cars on sale. The Chevrolet Corvair Monza Spider (already described) was the pioneer, but the Oldsmobile F85 Jetfire was launched almost immediately afterwards. The Jetfire was only built in 1962 and 1963, then dropped as Detroit reverted to its old axiom of 'there's no substitute for cubic inches' – larger engines instead of technical complexity taking over once again.

The Oldsmobile F85, along with its sister cars the Buick Special and the Pontiac Tempest, were the second series of 'compacts' put on sale by General Motors; the Chevrolet Corvair had been first, a year earlier. Not only were these cars significantly smaller than other GM cars but they were technically more advanced; the Pontiac pioneered the use of a 'rope drive' propeller shaft, located its transmission at the rear and used independent rear suspension.

Like other GM cars of this period the F85 was powered by a brand new light-alloy V8 engine of 215 CID/3.5 litres. In normally aspirated form this produced 155bhp (SAE), and was praised for its light weight and great reliability. Some innovations however are not readily accepted, and after only three years GM dropped it in favour of cast iron units and eventually sold the design rights to Rover of the UK, who went on to supply it for cars as different as the 3500 hatchback, the Range Rover, the Triumph TR8 (sold only in the United States) and the Morgan Plus 8.

In the spring of 1962, as a 'top of the range' edition of its F85 model, Oldsmobile upgraded the bucket-seat Cutlass coupé style by fitting a turbocharged version of the light-alloy V8, and called it the F85 De Luxe Jetfire. However, the technology was still too new for the cars to be completely reliable, and only 9,607 such coupés were produced before the car was dropped in the summer of 1963.

GM had already done a great deal of fundamental research into turbocharging (along with the American company Garrett) before committing itself to this engine. When finalized for production use, this first-generation turbo was mounted on top of the inlet manifold between the banks of the V8 engine, having already drawn its fuel-air mixture through the Carter carburettor mounted above the left-side cylinder bank. Maximum boost was 6 psi/0.4 Bar.

In this application, GM also provided an 'anti-detonation' system of fluid injection into the manifold downstream of the carburettor, but upstream of the turbo itself; this was a 50–50 mixture of methyl alcohol and water, used at the rate of about 8,000mpg.

By American standards the Jetfire was a fast car in its day, handling well and taxing its drum brakes to the limit. Unfortunately the potential clientele treated this new fangled engine layout with reserve, and did not buy as many cars as GM had hoped. Today such cars are extremely rare for the bodies tended to rust quite rapidly – a good survivor would be a real collector's piece for future generations to admire.

Oldsmobile's compact cars had grown somewhat by 1964 when this F85 Convertible was built. The turbocharged 'Jetfire' derivative – note the badge on the top of the facia crash roll, close to the base of the windscreen – (below) was meant to be a limited-production 'sports car' derivative of the range, and featured this special interior. The boost gauge was on the centre console ahead of the gear shift.

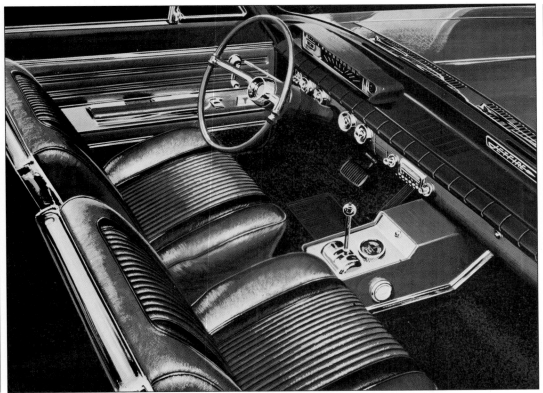

PEUGEOT 205 TURBO 16

PRODUCTION SPAN
1983 and 1984

ENGINE
4 cyl, Twin ohc

CAPACITY
108 CID/1,775cc

MAXIMUM POWER
200bhp (road car),
up to 450bhp (rally car)

CHASSIS/SUSPENSION
Steel unit-construction
body/chassis structure,
with tubular and
composite panels, coil
spring and wishbone ifs,
coil spring and
wishbone irs

BODY STYLE
2 door 2 seater saloon

TOP SPEED
(200bhp version)
130mph/208kph

0-60MPH
6.0 seconds

As with the Ford RS200 and the Lancia Delta S4, Peugeot greeted the new Group B motor sport category as the opportunity to create a completely new competition car. For lovers of technical novelty the glory of Group B was that every manufacturer seemed to have its own ideas about how to produce a specialized machine with a production run of only 200; Peugeot, like Lancia, decided to design a completely new car which would look as closely as possible like the 205 mass production model.

The new Group B Peugeot, eventually to become known as the 205 Turbo 16, was designed, developed, produced, refined and made into a winner in an astonishingly short time. Competitions director Jean Todt announced his intention to produce such a car in December 1981, the first prototype was running in the spring of 1983, the 200th car was built by the end of April 1984 and the first World Championship victory followed in August of that year.

Nor was it a flash in the pan. T16s won the World Rally Championship in 1985 and again in 1986, and a special version also won the famous Paris-Dakar marathon event in 1987.

Todt chose to clothe his new chassis design in a 205 body style for all the obvious marketing and publicity reasons, but except for a few common body panels there were virtually no common parts shared between the different cars. The T16 in fact had a four-cylinder, 16 valve, turbocharged, twin overhead-camshaft engine mounted transversely behind the two seats, and there was permanent four-wheel-drive. (The mass production 205 had a front-mounted engine, and front-wheel-drive).

The structure was sturdy and featured adjustable coil spring/wishbone independent suspension at front and rear, but most of the technical interest was in the engine and the transmission.

The engine was a new design drawn up around the cylinder block of a new generation of Peugeot engines (the XU range), and measured 108 CID/1,775cc; this, with the turbocharger 'factor' of 1.4 applied, meant that it fell neatly into the 153 CID/2.5 litre category.

It was conventional in every way – 16 valves, Bosch K-Jetronic fuel injection and twin-cams driven by an internally cogged belt – and was originally fitted with a KKK turbocharger at the rear (or side as installed in the car) of the engine. The rally engine was developed first, with 335/350bhp in its first season, but with 450bhp in Garrett turbocharged form for 1985; the engine fitted to the 200 'homologation' cars developed an easy 200 bhp at 6,750rpm.

The transmission was complex for the engine drove through a main gearbox mounted alongside it, the drive was then 'turned' through 90 degrees by bevel gears, and there were front, centre and rear differentials to make it all work.

Not only was the T16 an extremely successful rally car, but the road cars, except for a forgivable amount of transmission noise, were very fast, practical and versatile machines. Peugeot, unlike some of its rivals, had no trouble in selling all of them.

INSET Peugeot's 205 Turbo 16 was specifically designed as a turbocharged, mid-engined, four-wheel-drive, rally car, and it was amazingly successful. Its first big win came in 1984, but the 'works' team dominated the World Rally Championship series in 1985 and 1986.

RIGHT All the drama of Group B rallying, 1986-style, with the second version (called 'Evolution Two') of the Peugeot 205 T16 in full flight. In three seasons of rallying, the hugely powerful engines rarely gave trouble.

LEFT The engine of the 205 Turbo 16 was transversely mounted behind the seats, with the main gearbox on the opposite side of the car. In this view the large turbocharger is visible under the frame bracing tubes, with the exhaust pipe leading straight from it to the main silencer.

RIGHT The 205 Turbo 16 was so fast that it needed extensive aerodynamic work to keep it stable when 'flying'; note the large front chin spoiler, and the massive rear 'wing' above the tailgate.

BELOW Two versions of the 205, showing how the special turbocharged four-wheel-drive car looked like the mass-market 205, even though the two cars had little in common. The red car is the conventional front-drive 205, while the car liveried in Peugeot motorsport colours is the 205 Turbo 16 model.

PORSCHE 911 TURBO

PRODUCTION SPAN
Introduced in 1975

—

ENGINE
Flat 6 cyl, air-cooled, ohc

—

CAPACITY
183/201 CID–
2,994/3,229cc

—

MAXIMUM POWER
260/300bhp

—

CHASSIS/SUSPENSION
Steel unit-construction
body/chassis structure,
torsion bar and wishbone
ifs, torsion bar and
semi-trailing arm irs

—

BODY STYLE
2 door 4 seater coupé
cabriolet and 'Targa'
models

—

TOP SPEED
(300bhp version)
162mph/259kph

—

0 – 60 MPH
5.1 seconds

—

Ask the man in the street to name a turbocharged car, and the majority will probably answer 'Porsche'. That's a measure of the fame and charisma of the 911 Turbo which was not only one of the original breed, but has also been one of the longest-lasting and most successful types of turbocharged car.

The story of the 911 really dates back to the development of Porsche itself. The original Porsche sports cars were rear-engined machines closely based on the design of the (Porsche-designed) VW Beetle family. The next generation of Porsches, soon to become the legendary 911 series, was different in every detail, but stayed faithful to the first car's layout – the engine was air-cooled, was mounted in the tail and drove the rear wheels.

Early 911s, sold from 1964, had 122 CID/2.0 litre flat-six engines, but by the early 1970s they had gradually grown to 183 CID/3.0 litres. Racing Porsches used turbocharged versions of this durable and versatile unit in the early 1970s, and by the time that BMW launched its own pioneering 2002 Turbo road car, in September 1973, Porsche was well on its way to putting a turbocharged road car on sale.

The first Porsche 911 Turbo (the factory's internal project code for the engine was 930, by the way, but let's not confuse the issue) went on sale in 1975. It produced 260bhp and had so much torque (254lbft/35mkg) that it needed a new and stronger gearbox which only had four forward gears.

The 911's chassis was already well proven (though Porsche not only increased wheel and tyre widths, but provided new aerodynamic spoilers to optimize high speed stability), and as you might expect the turbocharged installation was carefully thought out. As on the normally aspirated Carreras Bosch fuel injection was retained, but the compression ratio was dropped from 8.5:1 to 6.5:1, maximum boost was 11.75 psi/0.8 Bar, the KKK turbocharger was located behind the engine, tucked down between the cylinder barrels the body panels and the transverse silencer – there was no intercooler at first.

With a 153mph top speed and the ability to sprint from rest to 100mph in 14.5 sec the original Porsche Turbo was an outstanding machine. Only two years later, from the autumn of 1977, it became quite phenomenal.

Not only was the engine enlarged to 201 CID/3,299cc, but an air-air intercooler was added to the specification (it was positioned under the rear spoiler), and the compression ratio was raised to 7.0:1. Peak power rose to no less than 300bhp and top speeds to more than 160mph.

Because it was so meticulously designed and developed the Porsche 911 Turbo was the most successful of all turbocharged cars. Even though the body style reached its public quarter century anniversary in 1988 there was no sign that its customers considered it out of date or not worth buying any more. The fact that a Porsche 911, because of its tail-heavy layout, was a difficult car to drive really fast did not seem to dissuade the customers either.

For all such reasons, and because it was the first of several different turbocharged Porsche cars, the 911 Turbo is probably the most important turbocharged car ever put on sale.

RIGHT When the 911 Turbo was designed, it was necessary to fit wider-rim wheels and fatter tyres, which necessitated the use of flared wheel arches, and those unmistakable lines were created. The engine was a flat-six air-cooled unit which was fitted in the tail, giving the car a rearward weight bias. In the late 1970s the 911 Turbo was one of the world's most glamorous cars, and still is.

BELOW RIGHT The original 911 shape was drawn up in the early 1960s, but was still attractive in the late 1980s. 911 Turbos not only had a 300bhp 3.3-litre turbocharged engine, but had a large 'duck-tail' spoiler to help trim the high-speed aerodynamic characteristics.

PORSCHE 924 TURBO

PRODUCTION SPAN
1979 to 1984

ENGINE
4 cyl, ohc

CAPACITY
121 CID/1,984cc

MAXIMUM POWER
170/177bhp

CHASSIS/SUSPENSION
Steel unit-construction body/chassis structure, coil spring and MacPherson strut ifs, torsion bars and semi-trailing arm irs

BODY STYLE
2 door 2+2 seater coupé

TOP SPEED
142mph/227kph

0-60MPH
7.7 seconds

For many years Porsche were happily settled into building cars with air-cooled engines mounted at the rear. Even though some people thought they were noisy and that they didn't handle very well, the cars sold in increasing numbers.

Then in the 1970s Porsche design philosophy changed completely. Two entirely different cars – the four-cylinder 924, and the V8 engined 928 – were announced, featuring water-cooled engines mounted at the front.

The 924 model was originally a project Porsche tackled on behalf of VW, who intended to sell the car with its own badging. Then, following the Energy Crisis of 1973 and a change of company management at the highest level, VW cancelled this car and Porsche decided to launch it under their own name. Although the body shell was newly designed by Porsche much of the running gear – engine, transmission and suspension – was adapted from components already in use at VW or Audi. Porsche arranged for the 924 to be assembled at the Audi factory at Neckarsulm, and launched it as a normally aspirated 125bhp car, at 'entry level' to the Porsche range.

Apart from those who complained that the 924 was 'not a real Porsche' many customers enjoyed driving the first front-engined car of that marque; but it was generally agreed that the chassis could accept a great deal more power. It was to satisfy those customers, and to fill a yawning gap between the 924 and the 911 models, that Porsche developed the 924 Turbo. Sales began in 1979 and the 924 Turbo was a success, even after it was effectively superseded by the larger engined 944. The two types were in production alongside each other for two more years.

Like the normal 924 the 924 Turbo had an overhead-cam 121 CID/ 2 litre four-cylinder engine mounted up front, with a combined transmission and final drive grouped at the rear. There was independent suspension at front and rear, disc brakes all round and generous 2+2 seating. Compared with the ordinary 924, style changes were confined to the use of different wheels, extra engine bay air intakes and extra front and rear aerodynamic aids.

The engine itself leaned over towards the right side of the engine bay. The KKK turbocharger was mounted low down and forward, quite hidden from view from above, behind and below the Bosch fuel injection system. For packaging purposes the turbo, with a maximum boost of 10 psi/0.7 Bar, drew air through the Bosch metering unit and the boosted air was then fed across the top of the engine to the throttle butterfly and inlet manifold, which was situated on the left side of the unit. There was no intercooler.

In comparison with the basic 924, the 924 Turbo was a much faster car; in addition to its spirited straight-line performance it also had a comfortable ride and excellent, well-balanced, roadholding. More than 5,000 were sold in 1980, and nearly 4,000 in 1981.

For a short time (in 1980 and 1981) it was joined by the limited-production 924 Carrera and Carrera GTS, of which a mere 456 were produced for competition purposes. Not only were these considerably more powerful derivatives of the Turbo – they had 210 bhp, aided by an intercooler. They had flared wheel arches, and a different nose, and were actually forerunners of the 944s in style. Such cars were fiercer and less civilized than the ordinary 924 Turbos, but were useful racing coupés with top speeds of more than 150mph.

RIGHT The happy marriage of form and function in one component – the cast alloy wheels of the 924 Turbo.

BELOW Compared with the 911 Turbo, the 924 Turbo was a discreetly styled 2+2 seater coupe. The engine was a four-cylinder unit mounted at the front, with the transmission at the rear.

PORSCHE 944 TURBO

PRODUCTION SPAN
Introduced in 1985

ENGINE
4 cyl, ohc

CAPACITY
151 CID/2,479cc

MAXIMUM POWER
220bhp

CHASSIS/SUSPENSION
Steel unit-construction
body/chassis structure,
coil spring and
MacPherson strut ifs,
torsion bars and semi-
trailing arm irs

BODY STYLE
2 door 2+2 seater coupé

TOP SPEED
153mph/245kph

0-60MPH
6.0 seconds

Once Porsche has introduced a brand new model, a lengthy and dedicated development process begins. Accordingly the 924, newly launched in 1975, was merely the first of many exciting cars to evolve from that basic layout.

Although the 924 family was originally damned with faint praise, as 'a good Audi coupé', the cars sold very well indeed. As already described, the turbocharged versions – 924 Turbo and 924 Carrera – were smart, fast and raceworthy machines.

Porsche soon went ahead with a much more ambitious project, which was to provide the 924 style of car with a new Porsche designed four-cylinder engine; this car was put on sale in 1981 and named the 944.

Basically the 944's new 151 CID/2.5 litre four-cylinder engine was related to that of the V8 unit fitted to the much larger Porsche 928, for it has the same general dimensions, overhead camshaft valve gear, and light alloy cylinder block and head. Because it was 'half of a V8' it was laid over at 45 degrees in the engine bay, and to make it as smooth as possible it was fitted with twin 'Lanchester' counter-rotating balancer shafts.

The structure itself was a further refinement of the flared wheel arch 924 Carrera style, on the same wheelbase as before, but with considerably wider tracks than that of the 924 model. Although it was still recognizably derived from the 924 it had a definite character and 'presence' all of its own.

The normally aspirated engine produced 163bhp, which was almost on a par with that of the 924 Turbo but with a more even spread of torque, so it was no surprise to see the 924 Turbo almost completely eclipsed by the new car.

Four years later however – things are never completed in an unseemly rush at Porsche – the company produced its next variation on the 924/944 theme, this being the modern masterpiece known as the 944 Turbo.

Naturally it had a turbocharged derivative of the engine, but there was a lot more change and improvement to the 944's design. The aerodynamicists had re-worked the shell yet again, adding yet another different nose and a carefully detailed lower aerofoil section under rather than over the tail. Brakes, suspension, transmission and facia instruments were all revised, the result being an even faster and more appealing package than the original car.

The new car's engine was a development of the 163bhp, two-valve version fitted to the normally aspirated 944, still installed at 45 degrees in the very full engine bay. The turbo arrangement however was very different from that built into the 924 Turbo. This time the water-cooled KKK turbocharger was mounted on the left side of the engine, under the inlet manifold, while the already occupied front end also included an air-air intercooler and an engine oil cooler.

Because it was a Porsche, every aspect of the car had been meticulously developed; the result was a phenomenally fast and civilized machine that handled beautifully. In the future, no doubt, it would be superseded, but in the late 1980s it set new standards in so many ways.

RIGHT The 944 Turbo looked superficially like the 924 Turbo, but was very different in detail. Not only was the styling subtly changed to incorporate the wider wheels and tyres, but there was a smoother nose with more air intakes to serve the 220bhp engine, and of course the engine was Porsche's own 2.5-litre 'four'.

LEFT The 944 Turbo's front corner featured hidden headlamps, extra driving lamps and turn indicators, all in the same wind-cheating area.

PORSCHE 956

GROUP C SPORTS CAR

PRODUCTION SPAN
1982 to 1985

ENGINE
Flat 6 cyl, Twin ohc

CAPACITY
162 CID/2,650cc

MAXIMUM POWER
620bhp

CHASSIS/SUSPENSION
Aluminium unit-construction body/chassis structure, coil spring and wishbone ifs, coil spring, lever arm and wishbone irs

BODY STYLE
2 door 2 seater racing coupé

TOP SPEED
240mph/384kph

0-60MPH
Not recorded

Porsche's first racing sports cars were built in the early 1950s, and the company has actively been involved in motor sport ever since then. The cars became progressively faster and more specialized as year followed year. By the 1970s every other sports car maker had to measure itself against the Porsches – usually by following them over the finish line.

The first turbocharged Porsche racing car was the 917–10 of 1972, an 800bhp monster with a 330 CID/5.4 litre flat-12 engine used in North American Can-Am racing. To follow this, Porsche developed a series of turbocharged versions of the flat-six air-cooled 911 engine, the most advanced of all having four-valve twin-cam cylinder heads with water cooling. A few years earlier a water cooled Porsche engine would have been considered heretical, but by the late 1970s it was expected.

Porsche then decided to build a single seater race car for the American 1980 Indy 500 race, choosing to develop a twin-cam four-valves-per-cylinder 162 CID/2.65 litre version of the famous flat-six engine, having water-cooled cylinder heads and air-cooled cylinder barrels. Unhappily for Porsche a change of regulations made the car ineligible for competition and the project was abandoned.

At first it looked as if all the work on this engine had been wasted. In 1982 however a new sports car racing formula – Group C which included fuel consumption limitations – gave Porsche the opportunity to build a new car for which this light, powerful, and fuel-efficient engine would be ideal. The result was the birth of the Porsche 956, a beautiful and wickedly fast two seater sports coupé which dominated world class sports car racing from the moment that it started its first event.

Except that it was the first racing Porsche sports car to use an aluminium monocoque structure instead of the multi-tube chassis frame which had been used for so long, the Type 956 was familiar to all racing enthusiasts. The engine/transmission package was placed amidships, behind the tiny cockpit, and the seating position was so far forward that the driver's feet were actually ahead of the line of the front wheels.

Although the flat-six engine was tenuously linked to that still used in the 911 Turbo road car, it was effectively a completely special racing unit. Because of the layout of the car, which was very wide, and because the engine was a flat-six, there were twin turbochargers. Each was mounted wide in the chassis, ahead of the line of the rear wheels, close to the intercoolers and water radiators.

Although it would have been possible to extract a lot more power from the engine, for the 956 it was necessary to eke out the fuel allowances. Accordingly, for most endurance races the boost was limited to 17 psi/1.2 Bar, when peak power was around 620bhp, while for the Le Mans 24 Hours race this was reduced to 16 psi/1.1 Bar, and 'only' 590bhp.

The 956 won its first Le Mans race, and almost every other long-distance sports car race for which it was entered in the next three seasons. Its successor, the 962, had a longer wheelbase and even more power than before; some race cars had enlarged, fully water-cooled, engines.

Porsche's 956 was a specialized Group C two-seater race car, complete with mid-mounted flat-six engine, and twin turbochargers. It was quite invincible for years, particularly in the Le Mans 24 Hour race, where its combination of speed and reliability was unbeatable.

PORSCHE
959

PRODUCTION SPAN
Introduced in 1985
–

ENGINE
Flat 6 cyl, Twin ohc
–

CAPACITY
174 CID/2,850cc
–

MAXIMUM POWER
450bhp
–

CHASSIS/SUSPENSION
Steel unit-construction
body/chassis structure,
alloy and composite
skin panels, coil spring
and wishbone ifs, coil
spring, lever arm and
wishbone irs
–

BODY STYLE
2 door 2 seater coupé
–

TOP SPEED
196mph/314kph
–

0-60MPH
3.7 seconds
–

Once Porsche engineers decide to tackle a particular project, they always make a proper job of it. This explains why the company's first four-wheel-drive car, the 959, was conceived in the early 1980s, unveiled as a Group B design study in 1983, nominally promised for first deliveries in 1985, yet did not actually begin to reach its customers until the end of 1987. Along the way the 959 had been turned from an out-and-out competition car into a thoroughly developed and environmentally 'clean' supercar.

One thing however did not change. In the beginning Porsche said it would build only 200 such cars – to achieve Group B homologation – and that aim has never been revised.

The roots of the 959 project lie in the famous 911, though precious few links except a generally similar profile, some body panels and a rear engine position remained by the time the 959 was ready for sale. The 911 course had a flat-six air-cooled engine mounted in the car's tail and driving the rear wheels.

The original 959 project featured a much modified 911 monocoque structure in which the drive line had been converted to provide four-wheel-drive. 'Works' cars built to contest the Paris-Dakar rally in 1984 were simple 911 conversions. This was good enough to win, but for 1985 and 1986 true 959 prototypes were built for the same event – and they also won in the latter year.

The 959 was not fully developed before Group B was cancelled, so definitive production cars were much more luxuriously furnished, as road going supercars, than might otherwise have been expected. Still loosely based on the wide-track 911 Turbo's body shell the 959 featured a smoother front end, a wrap-over rear spoiler and considerable sill/'running board' extensions along the flanks. The drag coefficient was only 0.32.

The engine was a developed version of that used in the 956/962 race cars and featured a mixture of water-cooling for the cylinder heads and air-cooling on the cylinder barrels. The 959 engine however featured twin KKK turbochargers and two intercoolers. The turbochargers worked in series, not in parallel, with one pulling strongly from low revs, the other chiming in at full throttle and high engine revs.

Such was the engine's efficiency that even with a maximum boost of 144 psi/1.0 Bar, and running on 95 Octane fuel, the 'road' engines cranked out an impressive 450bhp at 6,500rpm. For competition use the engine could be tuned to produce between 650 and 700bhp, while maintaining the sort of reliability for which Porsches are noted.

The 959 had a very sophisticated four-wheel-drive system, with a six-speed main gearbox and electronic monitoring and control of limited slip devices in the drive line. With the aid of fat tyres, an ABS anti-lock braking system and power-assisted steering, the 959's cornering power and general stability and security were probably better than those of any other car in the world – and it was one of the fastest too. It was no less than one could expect from Porsche, and it was going to be a real privilege to own one.

But if Porsche could do this in the 1980s, what might the 1990s bring?

RIGHT Only Porsche at its technically most adventurous could have produced the 959. The 911/959 lineage is clear. It had four-wheel-drive with electronic sensors and controls, and a massively powerful flat-six engine with twin turbochargers. The 'standard' car developed 450bhp, but up to 700bhp was possible in competition trim.

BELOW RIGHT In the beginning, the 959 evolved from the structure of the rear-engined 911, but by the time deliveries began in 1987 very few 911 parts remained. Only 200 959s were scheduled to be built – which was certain to make this one of *the* collectors' cars of the 1980s.

RANGE ROVER TD

PRODUCTION SPAN
Introduced in 1986
-
ENGINE
4 cyl, ohv
-
CAPACITY
146 CID/2,393cc
-
MAXIMUM POWER
112bhp
-
CHASSIS/SUSPENSION
Steel chassis frame,
with steel and light-alloy
body shell, coil spring
and radius arm front
beam, coil spring and
radius arm rear beam
-
BODY STYLE
4 door 5 seater estate car
-
TOP SPEED
90mph/1144kph
-
0-60MPH
18.1 seconds
-

Immediately after the end of the Second World War the Rover company designed a versatile four-wheel-drive vehicle, the Land-Rover. Originally this was little better than a copy of the famous Jeep, but the design gradually became more and more specialized. More than twenty years later the company designed a completely different 4×4, a larger and faster machine pitched at a more affluent market sector. This was the Range Rover – first put on sale in 1970 and more popular than ever in the late 1980s.

The basis of the Range Rover design was a 100in/254cm wheelbase chassis, with beam axles front and rear, all powered by the (petrol-powered) alloy V8 engine for which Rover had bought the design rights from General Motors in the 1960s. Permanent (now more fashionably called 'full-time') four-wheel-drive was a feature, as was the large, elegant and nicely equipped interior.

Not only could the car achieve nearly 100mph, but it could also be driven very slowly over rough ground. It was the most capable cross-country vehicle in the world, even though most of its customers in Britain never tackled anything more difficult than wet grass at a point-to-point meeting, or perhaps a muddy lane between house and sporting estate.

For many years Range Rover sales were limited by production capacity – about 10,000 cars a year – so there was no need to make the car any more versatile than it already was, and all derivatives were powered by the same V8 engine.

In the 1980s however, Range Rover production capacity was expanded, and demand for a diesel powered version increased. This was particularly apparent from countries where diesel fuel was much cheaper than petrol. After trying for some time, without success, to convert the V8 engine to diesel (Perkins designed this 'Snowflake' derivative), the company was forced to search for another unit.

Coincidentally the Rover SD1 car had recently been fitted with diesel engines from the Italian VM company, so after a European-wide search Range Rover also linked up with the same company. The engine chosen was a turbocharged four cylinder 146 CID/2.4 litre unit (basically the same as that fitted to the Rover private car). It produced 112bhp, which compared well with the 128bhp of the carburetted V8 petrol engine.

VM's engine was notable for the use of four individual cylinder heads. The compression ratio was no less than 22:1, the turbocharger was by KKK, with a maximum boost pressure of 12 psi/0.83 Bar, and there was an air-air intercooler mounted behind the radiator grille.

Range Rover and VM developed the engine so that the turbocharging effect did not begin to 'chime in' until the engine was pushed past 2,000rpm, so with peak power developed at only 4,200 rpm this felt like a relatively 'peaky' power unit. Some pundits complained that this made the TD a very sluggish machine at town speeds; on the other hand it had a very creditable top speed of 90mph, equal if not superior to any of its other four-wheel-drive rivals. Sales were confidently expected to exceed 2,000 a year.

The Range Rover was launched in 1970, and apart from minor facelifts was still being built in the same form in the late 1980s. With four-wheel-drive, high ground clearance and light alloy bodywork it was amazingly versatile. With optional turbocharged diesel power it was even more suitable for some markets.

INSET The Range Rover TD used a four-cylinder turbocharged VM engine, of Italian manufacture, similar to that used in the Rover 2400 SD Turbo private car. It featured individual cylinder heads – one for each cylinder.

LEFT No question of a stripped-out, utilitarian, interior for *this* diesel-engined car. The Range Rover TD was just as up-market as every other version of this four-wheel-drive range.

RIGHT Perhaps the turbo-diesel Range Rover was not as fast as its petrol-engined counterparts, but it was still a spacious and incredibly nimble four-wheel-drive estate car.

BELOW RIGHT The Range Rover has always had completely timeless, elegant styling, and all versions used the same 100in wheelbase. Almost all late-1980s examples had four passenger doors.

RENAULT 5 TURBO

PRODUCTION SPAN
1980 to 1985

—

ENGINE
4 cyl, ohv

—

CAPACITY
85 CID/1,397cc

—

MAXIMUM POWER
160bhp

—

CHASSIS/SUSPENSION
Steel unit-construction
body/chassis structure,
alloy and composite
panels, coil spring and
wishbone ifs, coil spring,
and wishbone irs

—

BODY STYLE
2 door 2 seater saloon

—

TOP SPEED
125mph/200kph

—

0-60MPH
6.5 seconds

—

As every Renault enthusiast knows, there was a world of difference between cars known as 5 Turbo and those named 5 GT Turbo. The 5 GT Turbo was merely a turbocharged version of the mass produced front-engined cars, while the 5 Turbo was a specialized mid-engined machine which just happened to look like a Renault 5!

During the 1970s Renault's production car rallying efforts had been hampered by the lack of a suitable car, so for the 1980s the company chose to alter that situation. Existing front-engined/front-wheel-drive cars had always been hampered by a lack of power, and a lack of traction. Renault engineers, being logical-thinking Frenchmen, therefore set out to design a car which could be an outright winner at World Championship level.

For all the obvious publicity and marketing reasons it was decided that the new design would be based on the general shape and basic structure of a front-engined 5, though by the time the design process had been finished only some structural and inner pressings remained from the original.

The key to the design was the use of a mid-mounted engine (placed where the rear seat of the hatchback should have been) which drove the rear wheels. That solved the traction problem, and Renault was confident that it could also tame the handling of a car which had about 60 per cent of its weight over the rear wheels.

To produce competitive power outputs Renault decided to fit a relatively small engine, but to turbocharge it. That chosen was the Renault 5 Gordini unit of 85 CID/1.4 litres, turbocharged and given a sizeable intercooler. In road car form this was set up to provide 160bhp, but in 'works' rally car tune it produced no less than 265bhp – or 190bhp/litre.

The five-speed gearbox/transaxle was a modified version of that used in the large Renault 30 executive hatchback. There was all-round independent suspension and four-wheel disc brakes. The original road cars had 13.3in/340mm diameter front wheels, and 14.4in/365mm diameter rear wheels, which soon proved to be too small for use in rallying. A later derivative, dubbed 'Turbo 2', used larger diameter wheels in rallies and was significantly more competitive.

The specially modified engine featured a cross-flow cylinder head. The exhaust manifold swept around the rear of the block to the Garrett T3 turbocharger which was under, but close to, the inlet manifold. A large air-air intercooler supplied boosted air direct to the inlet manifold, and the installation was completed by Bosch K-Jetronic fuel injection. Renault claimed that the intercooler, which was large by any standards, was worth up to 40bhp in a competition car.

Surprisingly enough, this well filled engine bay was kept cool merely by scooping air in through louvres behind each door, and there were hot outlets above and behind each wheel arch. The R5 Turbo sold well in France – well over 1,000 cars were sold – and seemed to be as much at home on the Champs Elysée as in the snow and ice of the Monte Carlo Rally. It died in 1985, soon after the second generation R5 came on sale.

RIGHT Renault set out to build a world-beating rally car in the late 1970s, and although it looked somewhat like the front-engined 5 model, it was mechanically unique, with a mid-mounted and turbocharged engine and rear-wheel-drive. Air intakes ahead of the rear wheels were needed to keep the high-output turbocharged engine cool.

BELOW RIGHT This model is a 'Turbo 2', with larger diameter wheels than in the original design. The improved roadholding which resulted made the car much more competitive when rallying.

RENAULT 5 GT TURBO

PRODUCTION SPAN
Introduced in 1984

—

ENGINE
4 cyl, ohv

—

CAPACITY
85 CID/1,397cc

—

MAXIMUM POWER
120bhp

—

CHASSIS/SUSPENSION
Steel unit-construction
body/chassis structure,
coil spring and
MacPherson strut ifs,
torsion bar and trailing
arm irs

—

BODY STYLE
3 door 4 seater saloon

—

TOP SPEED
120mph/192kph

—

0-60MPH
7.3 seconds

—

It would be easy to become confused by the various turbocharged Renault 5s but, as already explained the Renault 5 Turbo was a mid-engined rear-wheel-drive car, while all others had front engines and front-wheel-drive.

The Renault 5 hatchback was launched in 1972, with a variety of longitudinally mounted four-cylinder engines mounted behind the line of, but driving, the front wheels. For a while this was a strictly utilitarian range of cars, but the image perked up in 1976 with the launch of the R5 Alpine (which, perversely enough, was badged as a Gordini in the UK because another make of car was already using the 'Alpine' badge). The Alpine then gave way to the Alpine (Gordini) Turbo for 1982, with 110bhp instead of 93bhp from the same size of engine.

In the autumn of 1984, the second-generation Renault 5, known in France as the *Super-Cinq* was revealed. Although the latest car really looked like a slightly cleaned up version of the original, it was entirely different under the skin, and had been the subject of an enormous development programme. The single basic difference between the old and the new as that the new car finally fell into line with the majority of the world's compact hatchbacks, by fitting transversely-mounted engines and MacPherson strut front suspension.

As expected, there was to be a wide choice of engines, spanning 58 CID/956cc and 42bhp, to a turbocharged 85 CID/1.4 litre model with 120bhp, plus diesel engined options, and three-door or five-door styles.

The 5 GT Turbo aimed to fill the same market sector as the Alpine/Gordini Turbo which it replaced, for it was virtually the same size, weight and had a little more performance. Compared with the first-generation Renault 5s these cars were smoother and more wind-cheating, but still had wheel spin and cheeky characteristics which endeared them to the young French drivers.

The GT Turbo's engine, being transversely mounted in a very compact engine bay, was a tight fit. Like the engine in the first generation turbocharged car, and indeed that fitted to the limited production mid-engined 5 Turbo, it was based on the ubiquitous 85 CID/1,397cc four-cylinder unit which was used in so many other Renaults, but it had the high performance Gordini cylinder head with opposed valves.

Unlike the mid-engined car the 5 GT Turbo used only a tiny Garrett T2 turbocharger which was mounted at the end of the engine (towards the side of the engine bay) close to a small air-air intercooler crammed in to the left of the water radiator. Instead of fuel injection there was a Solex carburettor mounted above and behind the engine. Peak boost was 10.3 psi/0.72 Bar.

Compared with 1970s Renault 5s this was a very complex and tight fitting engine, but it was very effective and gave the car a great deal of performance and character. The performance was matched by eager steering and roadholding, and in every way this made the small Renault a latter-day Mini-Cooper. During 1987 it was made even more overtly sporting by a body face-lift, which made it appear more boisterous than ever.

Renault's 5GT Turbo of the late 1980s was the latest of a line of fast little sports hatchbacks. The first turbocharged Renault 5, called Gordini (or Alpine in the French market) went on sale in 1982, and the second-generation GT Turbo followed it in 1984. The turbocharged engine drove the front wheels, and gave the little car a top speed of 120mph, with scintillating acceleration.

SAAB 99/900 TURBO

PRODUCTION SPAN
Introduced in 1977

-

ENGINE
4 cyl, ohc/Twin ohc

-

CAPACITY
121 CID/1,985cc

-

MAXIMUM POWER
145/175bhp

-

CHASSIS/SUSPENSION
Steel unit-construction
body/chassis structure,
coil spring and wishbone
ifs, coil spring and
radius arm rear beam

-

BODY STYLE
2, 3, 4 or 5 door 5 seater
saloon or hatchback

-

TOP SPEED
117mph/187kph
(124mph/198kph with
175bhp engine)

-

0-60MPH
9.1 seconds (8.5 seconds
with 175bhp engine)

Saab is a Swedish company originally founded to build civil and military aircraft. The original Saab car was conceived soon after the Second World War. Like all Saabs ever built it had a front-mounted engine with front-wheel-drive. Early Saabs had two-stroke engines but from 1966 a Ford-Germany V4 engine was used instead.

A new generation of Saabs, the 99 range, went on sale in the late 1960s, at first with engines built by Triumph. Saab's own engine, a 121 CID/1,985cc four-cylinder unit with overhead camshaft valve gear, was finally made available in 1972.

In the meantime Saab was selling more and more of its products in the United States. As that country's exhaust emission regulations became progressively more strict, Saab saw that it would be difficult to maintain a competitive power output from the existing engine and searched for ways around the problem.

Original engines had a single carburettor, later units had twin carburettors, and finally Bosch fuel injection was adopted. This raised the power output to 118bhp, but it was not enough, and there was little chance of enlarging the engine within the confines of the existing cylinder block. Saab's philosophy was therefore to keep the same basic 121 CID/2 litre engine, but to improve volumetric efficiency by turbocharging it.

The first ever Saab Turbo was seen in prototype form in 1976, and sales began a year later. It was important not only because it changed Saab's own image (for the 99 Turbo was a real sports saloon), but also because it was the very first quantity production turbocharged touring car to be made anywhere in the world. BMW's 2002 Turbo had been a flop, Porsche's 911 of 1975 was a supercar and the TVR Turbo of 1976 was a limited production machine. The Saab was the first to make turbocharging respectable in terms of mass production.

Saab's engine was installed up front, leaning over to the right side of the engine bay at an angle of 45 degrees, and because the cylinder head had cross-flow breathing it wasn't easy to install the turbocharger. The turbo unit itself was positioned ahead of the engine, close to the exhaust ports, with fresh air drawn in from the other side and pressurized air returned to that other side. The turbo was a Garrett AiResearch unit, blowing at a maximum of 10 psi/0.7 Bar, and the whole engine was tuned so that the turbo began to have an effect from very low engine speeds. As a package it was, and is, a very neat installation.

Over the years the original 145bhp/single-camshaft installation went into many different Saabs, including the 99 and the longer wheelbase 900s. Then, in 1983, Saab unveiled the next generation of this amazing engine design, a twin-cam 16-valve unit complete with turbocharging and an intercooler.

The result was that the engine breathed even better than before, with cooler air being pushed into the engine; peak power was well up, from 145bhp to 175bhp. This was the engine of the mid-1980s 900 Cabriolet and it was also adopted as the most powerful unit used in the later 9000 Turbo model.

RIGHT After the BMW 2002 Turbo, the Saab Turbo was Europe's next turbocharged production car, first as the 99 and (from 1978) as the longer-wheelbase 900 range. Not only was the Saab a fast and well-balanced front-wheel-drive car, but it was also immensely safe and secure. Saab was still developing and evolving its 2-litre engine in the late 1980s, not only with the aid of turbocharging, but with 16-valve twin-cam cylinder heads, and sophisticated anti-knock controls.

INSET Both the Swedish manufacturers, Saab and Volvo, combine speed with style, and safety. The Saab's front-end style looked right, was efficient, and passed – indeed, surpassed – every regulation, anywhere in the world.

SAAB 9000 TURBO

PRODUCTION SPAN
Introduced in 1984

—

ENGINE
4 cyl, Twin ohc

—

CAPACITY
121 CID/1,985cc

—

MAXIMUM POWER
175bhp

—

CHASSIS/SUSPENSION
Steel unit-construction
body/chassis structure,
coil spring and
MacPherson strut ifs,
coil spring and radius
arm rear beam

—

BODY STYLE
5 door 5 seater hatchback

—

TOP SPEED
138mph/216kph

—

0-60MPH
8.3 seconds

—

Saab has always been noted for getting the most out of one model range before introducing the next. It was ten years before the Saab 99 was joined by the 900 (which was only a longer wheelbase re-design anyway) and six more years elapsed before the radically new 9000 range appeared.

Saab in the meantime had entered into a co-operative agreement with Fiat-Lancia. The new 9000, Lancia's new Thema and the forthcoming Fiat Croma thus had certain technical similarities and some body panels in common. Saab however did not share any running gear with the Italian cars, and by the time the cars were launched all co-operation had ceased.

Except that Saab was committed to using front-wheel-drive and a development of its existing 121 CID/2.0 litre four-cylinder engine, the 9000 was completely different from the 900 model. Not only was it larger and longer in the wheelbase, with MacPherson strut front suspension, but the engine was transversely positioned and leaned forward toward the nose of the car. There was a new five-speed gearbox bolted to the end, rather than the underside, of the cylinder block. There was no automatic transmission option at first, though the four-speed ZF automatic was made available for the 1987 model year. All in all the 9000 was a more spacious and more ambitiously specified, machine.

Saab always admitted that it intended to offer the 9000 model with a variety of engine tunes, but the first car to be put on sale carried the name of 9000 Turbo 16. Saab-watchers immediately realised that this indicated the use of the same 175bhp turbocharged twin-cam unit which had been revealed in 1983, and which was already being used in the smaller bodied 900 Turbo 16 car.

Because the 9000 had a transversely-mounted, rather than an in-line, engine, many details were different. In particular, the 9000's intercooler was very large indeed, and was fitted ahead of the water-cooling radiator at the front of the car. As with the more recent 900 Turbos, there was Saab's own APC system, a form of boost control which depended on detonation knock-sensors to instruct electronic microprocessors to open the turbo wastegate when the engine showed signs of distress; this attention to detail allowed the 'atmospheric' compression ratio to be relatively high (9.5:1), although peak boost from the Garrett T3 turbocharger could be as high as 12.3 psi/0.85 Bar. It was no wonder that Saab likened its modern cars to fighter aircraft (it was after all the manufacturer of the Viggen machine), especially as there was such a comprehensively equipped facia, including the discreet boost gauge.

Even though the 9000's engine, like all such turbocharged units, was a little breathless at low engine speeds, the turbo boost came in strongly but smoothly above about 3,000rpm, and this made the Turbo 16 derivative a very exciting car to drive hard. Because it had front wheel drive and there were limits to the amount of power that the tyres could handle, wheelspin could be provoked on tight corners and slippery surfaces.

In the late 1970s, Saab formed an alliance with Lancia of Italy, which explains why there was a distinct resemblance in style between its new 9000, and the Lancia Thema. All 9000s had front wheel drive, using an engine-over-gearbox configuration. The most powerful, also the first to be launched, was the 9000 Turbo. The 16-valve twin-cam engine developed no less than 175bhp.

TOYOTA CELICA TWIN-CAM TURBO

PRODUCTION SPAN
1983

ENGINE
4 cyl, Twin ohc

CAPACITY
128 CID/2,090cc

MAXIMUM POWER
320bhp in rally trim

CHASSIS/SUSPENSION
Steel unit-construction
body/chassis structure,
coil spring and
MacPherson strut ifs,
coil spring and radius
arm rear beam

BODY STYLE
2 door 2 seater coupé

TOP SPEED
Not recorded

0-60MPH
Not recorded

Toyota began making sporting cars in the early 1970s, and as its interest in motor sports grew so did the power and competitiveness of its sports coupés. A succession of Celicas were produced in the 1970s and 1980s; Toyota was always blessed with a wide range of engines from which to choose, some having twin overhead camshafts. A new generation of Celicas was launched in 1981 and the first turbo-charged engines were put on sale in 1982.

In the meantime Toyota's West German motorsport division was planning a car to use in the new Group B category. It would have liked to use four-wheel-drive to compete head-on with Audi, but was obliged to produce an improved version of the old front-engine/rear-drive chassis instead. This meant that the only way that the new rally car could be competitive was for it to be as strong as possible, and for it to have an extremely powerful engine.

A special version of the latest Celica, to be called Celica Twin-Cam Turbo, was therefore developed and 200 of these cars were produced during 1983. This model was never officially marketed in Europe, and it is doubtful if many were ever sold as pure road cars.

The basis of the new car was the Celica which had been launched in 1981, a car which had a rather square style and a very conventional 'chassis' with a beam rear axle. Visually the important change was that it had flared wheel arches, to allow wider wheels and tyres to be fitted. Other Celicas of this model family had engines varying from a 100bhp single-cam 1800 to a turbocharged 160bhp twin-cam (added to which there was also the long wheelbase, six-cylinder engined derivative called the Supra), but the Group B car had an entirely different engine.

To take advantage of Group B rules this was a turbocharged 128 CID/2,090cc four-cylinder unit: when the turbo 'factor' was applied, this put it near the top limit of the 183 CID/3.0 litre category. It still had only two valves per cylinder, but also had twin-overhead camshafts and a lengthy competitions history. In non-turbocharged guise this engine had been used in the late 1970s in a previous Celica model, when it produced no more than 200bhp in fully-tuned Group 2 guise.

The turbocharged version of 1983 used Nippondenso fuel injection, a KKK turbocharger and there was an intercooler up front. Maximum boost in rally form was 13 psi/0.9 Bar, this being quite enough to give the engine 320bhp, at which power it could reduce its rear (driven) tyres to shreds very rapidly indeed.

Like previous Celicas this was a very rugged, simply-engineered and reliable car, though clearly faster and more specialized than the other mass-production types. In spite of the compromise nature of its engineering, however, it was a very successful competition car, particularly in long-distance events like the Safari, Ivory Coast and Hong Kong – Beijing rallies.

RIGHT There have been many Toyota Celicas, in different shapes, and with different engines, but the Twin-Cam Turbo of 1983 was built for rallying. Under the angular coupe skin – which had flared wheel arches to accommodate widened wheels and tyres – there was a turbocharged 2.1-litre four-cylinder engine. In full rally car tune it developed more than 320bhp.

BELOW RIGHT The Celica Twin-Cam Turbo competition car had so much power that tyre wear was always a problem. Even so, the car was triumphantly successful in gruelling long-distance events like the Safari and Ivory Coast rallies.

TVR TURBO

PRODUCTION SPAN
1976 to 1979
—

ENGINE
V6 cyl, ohv
—

CAPACITY
183 CID/2,994cc
—

MAXIMUM POWER
230bhp
—

CHASSIS/SUSPENSION
Steel multi-tube chassis frame, with GRP body shell, coil spring and wishbone ifs, coil spring and wishbone irs
—

BODY STYLE
2 door 2 seater coupé, hatchback or convertible
—

TOP SPEED
139mph/222kph
—

0-60MPH
5.8 seconds
—

Trevor Wilkinson started building sports cars, in Blackpool in the 1950s, calling them TVRs. Twenty years on the company was still small, specialist and still building cars with multi-tube frames and GRP bodies. All of them used engines and transmissions bought in from mass-production manufacturers. Up to that point each and every TVR had been a two seater.

After various financial crises and management changes the company was revived by the Lilley family, father and son, in the late 1960s. Soon after this an entirely new range of TVRs, the M-Series models, were introduced; the original was unveiled in 1971 and before long a choice of three different engines – four-cylinder Ford, six-cylinder Triumph, and V6 cylinder Ford – were available. The ride was hard but the roadholding, braking and stability was excellent.

Because TVR was a small company it could react quickly to motoring fashion. During 1975 the company's managing director, Martin Lilley, saw the stir that was being caused by Porsche's new 911 Turbo and decided that TVR should also make such a car. At TVR though, time scales could be compressed, so the prototype was displayed in October 1975, with first deliveries being made in the following year.

At the time TVR's flagship was the 3000M model, a sleekly styled two-seater coupé fitted with the rugged but otherwise unexciting Ford-UK V6 engine of 183 CID/2,994cc; its power output was 138bhp and it was noted for its lusty low speed torque.

To develop this engine into an ultra-powerful turbocharged unit, TVR hired the British tuning company of Broadspeed. Broadspeed had already produced turbocharged versions of this engine, for possible use in the Ford Capri and Granada models, so the TVR contract was more of a re-packaging than a new design job.

TVR's turbo installation saw the Garrett or Holset turbocharger mounted ahead of the engine block, driven by the exhaust gases from both cylinder banks. Broadspeed retained the existing Weber carburettor, set maximum boost at 9 psi/0.62 Bar, completely rebuilt and 'blue-printed' the engine and claimed no less than 230bhp – which was a staggering 67 per cent improvement on the original.

Apart from an enlarged Salisbury 4HU final-drive unit with raised gearing, there were no other changes made to the sturdy chassis, the result being that the turbocharged TVR was a thoroughly exciting, red-blooded machine.

Because this was the very first turbocharged British production car road testers thought it was wonderful, and reports tended to be full of superlatives. To keep down the costs as far as possible TVR sold the Turbo as a conversion of existing models – coupé, hatchback or convertible – but even so the extra costs were very high. The result was that in four years only 63 such cars were produced, and when the next generation of TVRs, the Tasmin family, was launched in 1980 there was no turbo option. TVR have never put another turbocharged car on sale, preferring instead to offer cars with larger and ever larger engines.

RIGHT TVR was the first British manufacturer to offer a turbocharged car – actually as an engine option on any of its late 1970s models. This M-Series Coupe would normally be sold with a normally-aspirated Ford V6 engine of 138bhp, but in turbocharged form it pushed out a creditable 220bhp.

BELOW RIGHT All TVRs have been built around multi-tubular steel chassis frames, with glass-fibre bodies. This car, the Taimar hatchback version of the 3000M, was launched in 1977, and built until 1979. The turbocharged version was a very rare option: only 63 TVR Turbos of all types were ever built. They had shattering acceleration, and a 139mph top speed.

BELOW, FAR RIGHT The TVR Turbo had an intelligently designed and nicely furnished cockpit. There was a very good reason for the sturdy-looking tunnel between the seats – the multi-tube chassis surrounded the gearbox, with the upper tubes running towards the back of the car at that height.

VOLVO 760 TURBO

PRODUCTION SPAN
Introduced in 1982
-
ENGINE
4 cyl, ohc
-
CAPACITY
141 CID/2,316cc
-
MAXIMUM POWER
173/182bhp
-
CHASSIS/SUSPENSION
Steel unit-construction body/chassis structure, coil spring and MacPherson strut ifs, coil spring and radius arm rear beam, coil spring and wishbone irs for 1988
-
BODY STYLE
4 door 5 seater saloon or estate
-
TOP SPEED
120mph/192kph
-
0-60MPH
9.5 seconds
-

For many years Volvo was Sweden's most respected car maker, with a stodgy image for building safe but unexciting cars. This was only partly alleviated in the 1960s by the building of the P1800 family of sports coupés, and in the early 1980s by the offering of a turbocharged engine for the tank-like 240 models. The modern generation Volvos, dubbed the 760 range, were launched in 1982, and were originally seen as even more boring, and tank-like, than ever.

Although this new car looked as if it had been styled with a ruler, it was solidly built, demonstrably safe and secure. It was a heavy and ponderous car, about which no keen driver could ever get excited. Even when the car was launched, however, the development of a turbocharged version was mentioned, which arrived before the end of the calendar year. But there was a major surprise, for the press had been expecting to see a turbo version of the PRV V6 (which was to be used on several other European cars in the years which followed). Instead it was Volvo's own 'four' which was given the treatment.

The arrival of the 760 Turbo went some way to rescuing the car's reputation, though nothing could be done, until late 1987, about the bluff-nosed styling and the unimaginative rear suspension. It was at that point that the front was re-profiled, and made rather 'softer', and a complex independent rear suspension system was fitted.

The original 760 model was offered with a choice of a PRV-manufactured normally aspirated V6 or a VW-built turbocharged six-cylinder diesel. The 'sporting' petrol-powered turbocharged engine which followed was a development of that already in use in the old 240GLT model.

Volvo's own iron-blocked single-overhead-cam four-cylinder engine had been launched in 1974, as a thorough update of the ancient pushrod overhead valve engine that had been in use since the mid-1940s. By 1980 it had been enlarged to 141 CID/2,316cc and in normally-aspirated fuel-injected form it was producing 140bhp.

The turbocharged version introduced in 1980 was a typically cautious Volvo development, being a 130 CID/2.1 litre version producing a mere 155bhp; the engine planned for use in the 1980s-style 760 range was a more ambitious project.

The 760 Turbo's engine used the largest 141 CID/2.3 litre engine size, and had been redeveloped in detail. The turbocharger was a Garrett AiResearch T3 unit and was mounted close in to the cylinder block, pushing its air through a very large air-air intercooler on the way to the inlet manifold. The intercooler was mounted ahead of the normal water-cooling radiator and had its own electric cooling fan. Peak boost was only 8 psi/0.55 Bar, but this was matched to the high compression ratio of 9.0:1. In this guise no less than 173bhp was developed at 5,700rpm, this being increased to 182bhp a few years later.

The 760 Turbo was available in saloon or estate car form, with manual or automatic transmission, and soon took up a sizeable chunk of the 700-Series car's production of 30,000 cars a year.

RIGHT Volvo's 700 series range was introduced in 1982, and was expected to go on selling for many years. There were saloons and estate cars, diesel and petrol engines, of various sizes. The most powerful of all was the turbocharged four-cylinder 2.3-litre unit which, together with an intercooler, produced a peak of 182bhp. For 1988 the rather angular lines of the 760 were softened at the front, and at the same time the cars were given independent rear suspension.

BELOW RIGHT The first-generation 760s had very angular styling, and were often called 'battleships'. For 1988, this subtly rounded style, with slightly angled back nose, was adopted. Under the skin of this car was a powerful turbocharged engine which gave a top speed of 120mph.

RIGHT Volvo 760 facias were nothing if not functional. The turbo boost gauge was mounted neatly under the quadrant of the rev-counter.

MIDDLE RIGHT Ever since the 1920s, when the Swedish Volvo car was first launched, the same sort of badge has been retained. It calls forth an instant recognition of solid worth and unsurpassed reliability.

BOTTOM RIGHT Not many people would know what an intercooler actually does, but Volvo wanted the world to know that its 760 Turbo had one fitted. The intercooler, in fact, cooled down the pressurized air before it reached the engine, thus making it more dense, and consequently helping the engine to develop more power.

TOP LEFT Simple, but comprehensive, climate controls were fitted to the centre of the 760's facia/instrument panel.

ABOVE The 760 Estate's loading area could swallow a mountain of goods, children, dogs and luggage without straining anything more than the driver's nerves.

LEFT Modern engines, especially when turbocharged, do not encourage do-it-yourself maintenance efforts by their owners. Somewhere in there is a Volvo 760 Turbo engine, the turbocharger, the piping to the intercooler, and the potential to develop 182bhp.

INDEX

Page references to relevant captions are given in *italics*

A

Abarth: 62
ABS (anti-lock braking system): 26, *76*, 104
Alboreto, Michele: *38*
Alfa Romeo: *11, 13*
    8C2300: *8*
    Tipo B (P3): *13*
Alpine: *see* Renault
Alison: 13
Allanté: *see* Cadillac
Andretti, Mario: 60
A Plus engine: *82*
Aries: *see* Dodge
'A-Series' engine: 82
Aston Martin Tickford: 46, *48*
Audi: 8, *19*, 98, 118
    80 saloons: 16
    Audi-Volkswagen Iltis: 16
    Quattro Coupé: 16, *16, 18, 19*, 86
    Quattro Sport: 16
Austin-Rover: 82, *82*
    Metro: 82
    see also MG Metro; Rover
Australian Grand Prix:
    1987: *38*
Auto: *19*
Auto-Union family: *19*

B

'Beetle': *see* Volkswagen
Bentley: *see* Rolls-Royce
Berger, Gerhard: *38*
Biturbo: *see* Maserati
BL Cars (British Leyland): 82
    Mini: 82
    see also Austin-Rover; MG Metro; Rover
BMC: 82
BMW: 8, 22
    M1 coupé: 26
    745i: 26, *26, 29*
    7-series: 26, *26*
    Turbo show car: 22
    2002 Turbo: 8, 22, *22, 24, 25, 26*, 96, 114, *114*
    2800: 26
BMW (South Africa):
    745i: 26
Borg Warner transmission: 48, 80
Bosch: 46
    injection systems: 52, 88, 96, 98, 114
    KE-Jetronic injection system: 20, 44
    K-Jetronic injection system: 110
    L-Jetronic injection system: 34, 42, 74, 76
    multi-point fuel injection: 78

Brabham: 22
British Leyland: *see* BL Cars
British RAC International Rally (1985): 62, *62*
British Rallycross Grand Prix (1987): 52
Broadspeed: 8, 120
Buchi, Alfred: 13
Bugatti: *11, 13*
    Type 57: *11*
    Type 57SC: *11*
Buick: 8
    Special: 90

C

Cabriolet: *see* Saab
Cadillac Allanté: 32
Camaro: *see* Chevrolet
Can-Am Racing: 102
Capri: *see* Ford
Carrera: *see* Porsche
Carter carburettor: 90
CART-racing: *60*
Celica: *see* Toyota
Chapman, Colin: *68*
Chevrolet:
    Camaro 36, 56
    Corvair: 30
    Corvair (1965 version): 30
    Corvair Monza Spider: 8, 30, *30*, 90
    Corvette: *7*
    Corvette V8 engine: *7*
Chrysler: 30, 32, *32*, 36, 86
    Chrysler Maserati: 32, *32*, 36
    Laser Turbo: 32, 36
    see also Dodge
Citroen: 34
    CX25 GTI Turbo: 34, *34*
    DS19/21/23 series: 34
    SM-type gearbox: 68
Colt Starion: *see* Mitsubishi
Comprex BBC pressure-wave supercharging: 38
Constructors' Championship (1982): 38
Cooper: 60
Cortina: *see* Ford
Corvair: *see* Chevrolet
Corvair Monza Spider: *see* Chevrolet
Corvette: *see* Chevrolet
Cosworth Engineering: *50*
    BDA engine: 52
    BDT engine: 52, *54*
    BDT-E engine: *54*
    DFV engine: 38, 60
    DFX ('Indy') engine: 8, 60, *60, 61*
    see also Ford
Croma: *see* Fiat
Cutlass: *see* Oldsmobile

D

Datsun: *see* Nissan
Daytona Turbo: *see* Dodge
Dellis, Fred: 42
Dellorto DHLA carburettor: 68
DeLorean DMC12: 14
Delta: *see* Lancia
DeTomaso, Alejandro: 72, *72*
DeTomaso Pantera project: 32
DFX engine: *see* Cosworth Engineering
DKW: *19*
Dodge:
    Aries: 36
    Daytona Turbo: 32, 36, *36*
DTSS (Dynamic Tracking Suspension System): 76

E

ECI (Electronic Control Injection): 86
Escort: *see* Ford
European Touring Car Championship (1969): 22

F

Fagioli, Luigi: *13*
Fairlady: *see* Nissan
Ferrari: *38*, 62
    Dino 246GT: 40
    F1: 38-9, *38, 39*
    F40: 40
    GTO: 40, *40*
    GTO 'Evolution' version: 40
    GTO-type V8 engine: *7*
    308GTB: 40
Fiat: 8, 42
    Croma: 116
    124 Spider Turbo: 42, *42*
    124 Sport Spider: 42, 72
    Ritmo-Strada: 64
    see also Lancia
Fiat-Lancia: 116, *116*
Fiat-USA: 42
Firebird: *see* General Motors
Ford: *48, 74*, 120
    Capri: 46, 56, 120
    Capri Mk II: 46
    Capri Mk III: 46
    Capri 2.8i: 46
    Capri 2.8 Turbo: 46, *46 47*
    Cortina: 56
    Escort: 44, *54, 74*
    Escort Mk III: 44
    Escort RS 1600: 52
    Escort RS 1600i: 44
    Escort RS 1800: 52
    Escort RS Turbo: 44, *44*
    Escort XR3: 44
    Escort XR3i: 44, *44*

Granada: 120
Granada Scorpio: 48
Mustang: 44, 56, 58
Mustang SVO: 56, *56, 57*, 80
Mustang II: 56
Mustang III: 35, 44, 56
RS200: *52, 52, 54*, 62, 92
Sierra: *52*, 56, 58, 80
Sierra RS Cosworth: 12, 48, *48, 49, 50*
Sierra RS500 Cosworth: 48, *48, 49, 50*
Sierra XR4i: 56, 80, *80*
Tempo: 58
Thunderbird Turbo Coupé: 32, 56, 58, *58, 59*
see also Lincoln; Mercury; Merkur
Ford-Europe: 8, 44
Ford-Germany: 114
Ford-UK: 120
Ford-USA: 8, 30, 44, *56*, 80
Forghieri, Ing, Mauro: 38
Fulvia: *see* Lancia

G

Galant/Sapporo chassis: 86
Garrett AiResearch: 13, 90
TO3 turbocharger: 88
TO3/TO4 turbocharger: 52
TO4 turbocharger: 20
T2 turbocharger: 112
T3 turbocharger: 14, 44, 64, 68, 82, 110, 116
turbochargers: 32, 34, 36, 42, 48, 56, 78, 80, 114, 120, 122
General Motors: 8, 30, 90
Firebird: 56
Jeep: 106
see also Chevrolet; Oldsmobile

Geneva Motor Show (1984): 40
Ghia: 52, *52*
Giugiaro, Georgetto, *67*, 68, *68*
Gordini (car): *see* Renault
Gordini engine: 110
Granada Scorpio: *see* Ford
GRP (glass reinforced plastic): 14

H

Hitachi: 76
Holset turbocharger: 120
Hong Kong-Beijing Rally: 118
Horch: *19*

I

Iacocca, Lee: 32, *32*, 36
IHI turbochargers: 40, 46, 58, 72

RHB 5: 74
Indianapolis ('Indy') 500 race: 60
1980: 102
'Indy' engine: *see* Cosworth Engineering
intercooler: *124*
Italian Grand Prix:
1933: *13*
Ivory Coast Rally: 118, *118*

J

James Bond movies: *68*
Jeep: *see* General Motors
Jano, Vittorio: *8*
Jetfire: *see* Oldsmobile

K

Kankkunen, Juha: 64
Karmann: 80
K-Cars: 36
KKK turbochargers: 16, 22, 26, 46, 62, 96, 98, 100, 104, 106, 118
Kranefuss, Mike: 56

L

Lanchester shafts: 100
Lancia: 92
Delta: *67*
Delta hatchback: 62, 64
Delta HF 4WD: 64, *64, 67*
Delta S4: 52, 62, *62*, 64, *64*, 92
Fulvia: 62
Prisma: 64
Stratos: 62
Thema: 64, 116, *116*
037 Rally: 62
see also Fiat-Lancia
Land-Rover: *see* Rover
Laser Turbo: *see* Chrysler
Lauda, Niki: 40
Le Baron: 32
Legend Industries: 42
Le Mans 24 Hour Race (1982): 102, *102*
Lilley, Martin: 120
Lima engine: 8, 56, 58, 80
Lincoln: 56
Continental: 58
Mk VII: 58
Lincoln-Mercury division: 80
Lola: 60
Lotus: 8, 60, 82, *82*
Élite hatchback: 68
Ésprit: 68
Ésprit Turbo: 68, *68*

M

March: 60
Maserati: 8, *11, 32*
Biturbo: 72, *72*
see also Chrysler
Mazda: 74, 76
RX-7 2.6 Litre Turbo: 74, 76, *76*
RX-7 Savanna: 76
323 Turbo 4WD: 74, *74, 75*
Mears, Rick: 60
Mercedes-Benz: 8, 12, 32, 78
300SDL Turbodiesel: 78
300TD Turbo: 78, *78*
W124: 78
Mercury: 56
Cougar: 58
see also Lincoln-Mercury division
Merkur XR4Ti: 44, 80, *80*
Metro: *see* Austin-Rover; MG Metro
MGB: 42, *42*
MG Metro:
1300: 82
Turbo: 82, *82, 84, 85*
Mini: *see* BL Cars
Mitsubishi: 8, 86
Colt Starion: 86, *86*
Monaco Grand Prix:
1932: *11*
1981: 38
monocoque models:
Bentley Mulsanne Turbo R: 20
Fiat 124 Spider Turbo 124
Porsche 956 Group C Sports Car: 102
Porsche 959: 104
Monte Carlo Rally: 110
1986: 62, *62*
1987: 64
Monza: 30
see also Chevrolet
Morgan Plus 8: 90
Motor Trend: 58
Mulsanne: *see* Rolls-Royce
Mustang: *see* Ford

N

Nader, Ralph: 30
New Yorker: 32
Nippondenso fuel injection: 118
Nissan (Datsun): 8, 86, 88
Fairlady Z/300ZX 88, *88, 89*
Targa body: 88
280ZX: 88
Z-Cars: 88
Z31 series: 88
NSU: 76

O

Offenhauser engine: 60
Oldsmobile:
F85 De Luxe Jetfire: 8, 90, *90*

P

Paris-Dakar marathon
1984: 104
1986: 104
1987: 92
Pennzoil: *60*
Penske, Roger: *60*
Perkins: 106
Peugeot: 8, 14, 34, 92
205 Turbo 16: 52, 62, 92, *92, 95*
XU engines: 92
Pininfarina: 40, *40*, 42, *42*
Pinto engine: *see* T88/Pinto engine
Plastow, David: 20
Pontiac:
Tempest: 90
Porsche: 8, 38, 86, 96, 98, 100, 102, 104
Carerra GTS: 98
911 Turbo: 8, 14, 96, *96, 99*, 102, 104, *104*, 120
917 Turbo: 8
917-10: 102
924: 76, 98, *98, 99*, 100, *100*
924 Carrera: 98, 100
924S: 76
928: 98, 100
944: 76, 100, *100, 101*
956 Group C Sports Car: 102, *102*
959: 104, *104*
962: 102
Portuguese Grand Prix:
1987: *38*
Pratt & Whitney: 13
Prisma: *see* Lancia
PRV engine: 122

Q

Quattro: *see* Audi

R

Range Rover: *see* Rover
Reliant: 52
Renault: 8, *8, 14*, 38, 110
Alpine-Renault GTA V6 Turbo: 14, *14*
Alpine Turbo (Gordini Turbo): 112
A310: 14
5: 110

5 (second generation:
    Super-Cinq): 112
5 Alpine (5 Gordini): 112, *112*
5 Gordini: *see* Renault 5
    Alpine
5 Turbo: 110, *110,* 112, *112*
5 'Turbo 2': 110, *110*
5GT Turbo: 110, *110,* 112,
    112
Gordini Turbo: *see* Renault
    Alpine Turbo
Super-Cinq: *see* Renault 5
    (second generation) 25: 14
25 Turbo engine: 14
30: 110
Type 310: 14
Renix engine management
    system: 14
Ritmo-Strada: *see* Fiat
Rolls-Royce: 20
    Bentley Mulsanne Turbo: 8,
        20, *20*
    Bentley Mulsanne Turbo R:
        20, *20*
    Bentley T-Series: 20
    Mulsanne: 20
    Silver Shadow: 20
Rover: 90, 106
    Land-Rover: 106
    Range Rover: 90, *106*
    Range Rover TD: 106, *106,*
        108
    SDI: 106
    3500 hatchback: 90
    2400 SD Turbo: *106*
    Triumph engines: 114, 120
    Triumph TR8: 90

see also Austin-Rover
RS-type wheels: 46

S

Saab: 8, 44, 114, 116
    APC system: 116
    99 range: 114
    99/900 Turbo: 114, *114,* 116
    900 Cabriolet: 114
    9000: 116, *116*
    9000 Turbo: 114, 116, *116*
    ZF automatic: 116
Safari Rally: 118, *118*
Salisbury 4HU final-drive unit:
    120
Savanna: *see* Mazda
Sierra: *see* Ford
Smith, Martin: *18*
'Snowflake' engine: 106
Solex carburettor: 20, 112
Special: *see* Buick
Spider: *see* Fiat
Spyder: 30, *30*
    see also Chevrolet
Starion: *see* Mitsubishi
Stratos: *see* Lancia
superchargers: 10-12, 13
Super-Cinq: see Renault

T

Taimar: *see* TVR
Tasmin: *see* TVR
T-Bird (Thunderbird): *see* Ford

Tempo: *see* Ford
T88/Pinto engine: *50,* 58
Tempest: *see* Pontiac
Thema: *see* Lancia
Thunderbird: *see* Ford
Todt, Jean: 92
Torsen differential: 64
Toyota: 8, 88
    Celica: 118
    Celica Twin-Cam Turbo: 118,
        118
Treser, Walter: 16
Triumph: *see* Rover
turbochargers: 12-13 *et passim*
Turbo Lancer: 86
TVR: 120, *120*
    M-Series: 120, *120*
    Tasmin family: 120
    3000M: 120
    3000M Taimar hatchback:
        120
    Turbo: 114, 120, *120*

V

Vel's Parnelli Jones team: 60
viscous-coupling limited-slip
    differential: 44
VM: 106
Volkswagen (VW): 98, 122
    'Beetle': 30, 96
    see also Audi
Volumex superchargers: 62, 64
Volvo: 8, 14, *14, 114*
    P1800: 122
    700 series: 122, *122*

760: 14
760 Turbo: 122, *122, 124, 125*
240: 122
240GLT: 122
VW: *see* Volkswagen

W

Wanderer: *19*
Wankel, Felix: 76
Wankel rotary engine: 76
wastegate control: 13
Weber carburettor: 46, *46,* 72,
    120
Weber Marelli fuel injection: 48,
    50
Wilkinson, Trevor: 120
World Championship:
    1984: 92, *92*
World Rally Championship:
    1985: 92, *92*
    1986: 92, *92*
    1987: 64, *64,* 74
World Touring Car
    Championships:
    1986: *54*
    1987: *49*

Z

Zagato: 72
Zakspeed: 46
Z-Cars: *see* Nissan
ZF automatic transmission: 26

PICTURE CREDITS

Andrew Morland pp 6, 9, 10, 11 (top), 61 (below); J Baker Collection pp 8, 11 (below), 12, 13, 15, 17, 18, 19, 35, 71, 83, 84, 85, 97 (bottom), 107, 108, 109, 111, 123, 124, 125; Rolls-Royce Motors Ltd p 21; L & C Tunbridge Wells pp 23, 24, 25; BMW pp 27, 28, 29; GM Chevrolet pp 31 (middle and below); Collectible Automobile p 31 (top); Chrysler Corporation pp 33, 37; Ferrari pp 7, 38, 39, 41; Pininfarina p 43; Ford-UK pp 45, 49, 50, 51, 53, 54, 55, 81; Ford Germany p 47; Ford-USA pp 57, 59; Penske Racing p 61 (top); Lancia pp 63, 65, 66, 67; Lotus pp 69, 70; Maserati p 73; Mazda pp 75, 77; Mercedes-Benz p 79; Mitsubishi p 87 (top and below left); John McGovren p 87 (below right); Nissan p 89; National Motor Museum p 91 (top); Ludvigsen Library p 91 (bottom); Colin Taylor p 93; Peugeot pp 94, 95; Porsche Cars pp 97 (top), 99, 101, 103, 105; Renault p 113; Saab pp 115, 117; Toyota p 119; TVR p 121